MAKING TOYS IN WOOD

EDITED BY

CHARLES H. HAYWARD

Editor of
WOODWORKER MAGAZINE
Author of
Tools for Woodwork, Practical Veneering,
Light Machines for Woodwork, Garden
Woodwork, Woodwork Joints, Complete
Book of Woodwork, etc.

STERLING
PUBLISHING CO., INC. NEW YORK

Published in 1980 by
Sterling Publishing Co., Inc.
Two Park Avenue
New York, N.Y. 10016

© Evans Brothers Ltd. 1972, 1963 in England
First published in England in 1963 as Making Toys in Wood.
Published by arrangement with Evans Brothers Ltd.
This edition available in the United States, Canada and
the Philippine Islands only.

Library of Congress Catalog Card No.: 80-52591
ISBN 0-8069-8496-1
Previously:
ISBN 0-273-87749-061-9

CONTENTS

MAKING TOYS IN WOOD

DOLL'S BUNGALOW

A HOUSE OF this kind can be either covered with one of the printed doll's house papers in miniature of brick or stone, or it can be painted. The latter is in many ways preferable in that it gives far greater scope for artistic treatment and is much less mechanical looking. Those who feel put off by the rather regular horizontal lines of the brick work can paint imitation broken stone, the stones being of completely irregular form.

FIG. I. SOMETHING THAT WILL APPEAL TO EVERY GIRL
The suggested size of 2 ft. by I ft. 6 in. is quite big enough for the small houses of today though there is no reason why it should not be made bigger if the space is available

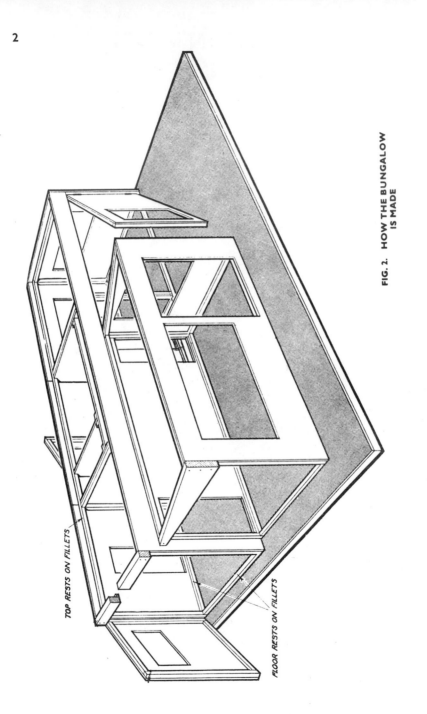

TOP RESTS ON FILLETS

FLOOR RESTS ON FILLETS

FIG. 2. HOW THE BUNGALOW IS MADE

Baseboard. This is a sheet of ply or hardboard mounted on a framework of solid wood about 3 in. by $\frac{1}{2}$ in. section. The frame can be mitred together and assembled with glue and nails. When the panel is fixed to it with glue and nails the whole is bound tightly together. Later the top edge is rounded as shown, but this should not be done until the positions of the walls have been plotted out.

Draw in the lines of the walls with pencil, noting those which are pivoted to give access. For the fixed walls there is no complication, but some of the hinged walls, notably those of the left-hand side, fit over the face (see Figs. 2 and 7). Consequently the fixed walls have to stop short. There is no difficulty, however, if the lines are plotted out on the actual baseboard.

The corner fillets can be $\frac{1}{2}$ in. by $\frac{3}{8}$ in. softwood. They are glued and pinned down on to the base. In some instances, for instance the interior walls, the nails will pass into the hardboard only, and for these it is advisable to reverse the board after the glue has set and clench the nails. Do not rely upon nails only.

Walls. The lengths of these are obvious from the lines on the baseboard. Note, however, that the height varies. Outer walls reach to the extreme top, but interior party walls are set down to enable the flat roof to be fitted over them. Note from Fig. 7 that top corner fillets are needed to hold the roof. They are fixed $\frac{1}{2}$ in. down from the top edge. The interior walls are thus $\frac{1}{2}$ in. lower than the others.

Cut out the walls, fitting them to the lines marked out on the base. Corner fillets have to be added to enable them to be fixed to each other, and the positions again are obvious from the baseboard. Window and door openings have to be fretted out, and it should be noted that the door openings stand up from the bottom, not only above the fillets, but also above the floors later to be laid. Thus, assuming the fillet to be $\frac{3}{8}$ in. thick, and the hardboard $\frac{1}{8}$ in., the opening will be $\frac{1}{2}$ in. from the bottom. Unless this is done there will be a gap between the floors where they meet at the door openings. The actual size should be calculated in accordance with the material being used. Glue and nail the fillets and assemble the walls to each other, and finally to the baseboard.

At the left-hand end two strips of solid wood are used at the top, that at the front being tapered to give the sloping roof. The hinged walls open beneath these. Make up the hinged walls complete, trim them to a generous fit, and hinge. The doors are best hinged with strips of tape glued along the edges and to the walls. It will be found stronger than attempting to use screwed-on or pinned metal hinges.

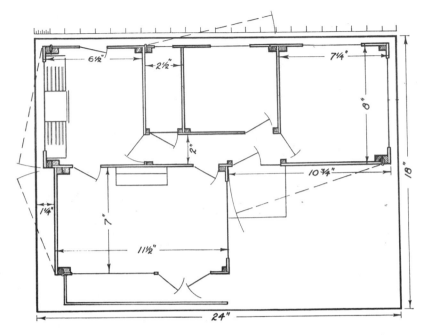

FIG. 3.   PLAN VIEW, ROOFS REMOVED

FIG 4.   FRONT VIEW SHOWING DOOR

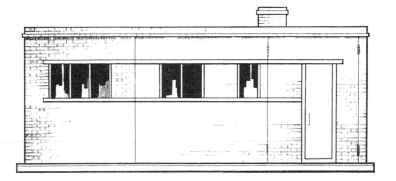

FIG. 5. BACK WALL

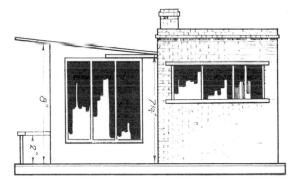

FIG. 6. RIGHT-HAND WALL

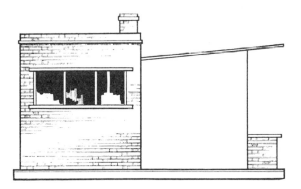

FIG. 7. LEFT-HAND WALL

Floors and roofs. Cut out the floors to rest upon the fillets, and fix down with glue and nails. Of the two roofs, the large one fits inside the walls on the fillets; the other lies on top. Neither should be fixed until all interior decorations have been completed, because otherwise it would be difficult if not impossible to reach certain parts. If preferred the large roof need not be fixed at all.

Fitting up. The simplest way of fixing the window glasses is to cut an outer frame in thin plywood or even cardboard and glue it to the outside of the walls. It should project inwards about $\frac{1}{8}$ in. to form a rebate in which the glass can fit from inside. The glass is held either by driving small pins into the rebate, leaving the hands projecting slightly, or by gluing round little strips of card. In fact a thin seam of *Seccotine* put round the edges of the glass and left to become tacky before putting in position is satisfactory without any other fixing. Where windows have small detail such as the bars of that adjoining front door it is simpler to paint them on the glass.

Many schemes are possible for the inside walls. Paints can be used, or suitable wallpaper can be stuck on. If special doll's house paper is not available ordinary wallpaper can be used if it has a small design. It is also possible to buy fancy wrapping paper, some patterns of which are quite successful. Those with the skill might consider making their own.

For carpets, etc., actual material might be used. Sometimes it is possible to obtain coloured catalogues which include carpets which could be cut out and stuck down. For a strip wood effect a sheet of veneer with lines drawn on it could be used.

Mantelpieces, wash basins, bath, etc., can be left to the ingenuity of the reader. Blocks of wood cut to shape and painted are quite effective. The same thing applies to the chimney stack which is a solid block. Pictures can be cut from magazines or books and frames painted around them.

Note that an applied strip is added near the top of the walls on the outside. It can be in card or thin wood, and is level with the roof. If the walls are to be painted a ground colour representing the bricks or the stone should be painted on first. It gives a more attractive appearance if the colour is varied somewhat. When dry the lines of the mortar seams can be painted in.

Material. The house takes about 20 sq. ft. of hardboard and can be cut from a sheet of 5 ft. by 4 ft. if care is taken in marking out economically. The nearest larger size should be selected, though it is often possible to buy small off-cuts which can be used.

TWO-SEATER TOBOGGAN

ALTHOUGH IN THIS country we do not get a lot of snow, at any rate in the South, most people enjoy a run on a toboggan. It is well worth making one so that it is ready for when there is a fall. That shown in Fig. 1 measures just over 5 ft. long and will hold two adults or three children at a pinch.

As the main runners are bent to give the curvature they should be made in a suitable hardwood such as beech which bends well. Alternatively ash or birch could be used. The nose piece to which they are fixed should be in a hardwood which is not liable to split. Elm is excellent in this respect, though other hardwoods could be used. Sides and seat slats could be in softwood.

The whole thing is painted to protect it from damp, but it is inevitable that the runners will become exposed with friction, even when metal facings are added. It is advisable to wipe them dry and keep the toboggan under cover when not in use.

Runners. Fig. 3 shows how each pair of runners fits into notches cut in the nose-piece. They are screwed in, but it is also advisable

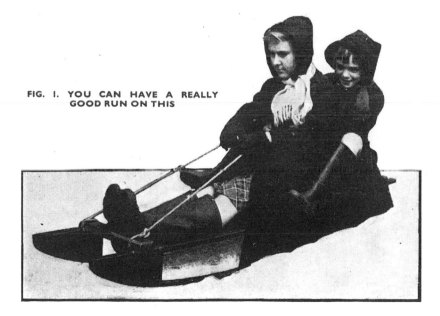

FIG. 1. YOU CAN HAVE A REALLY GOOD RUN ON THIS

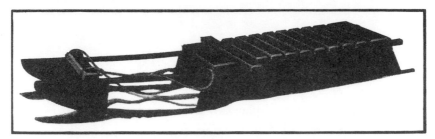

Fig. 2. COMPLETED TOBOGGAN. BOTH HARDWOOD AND SOFTWOOD ARE USED
Over-all length is just over 5 ft., though this could be adapted within a little

to use a water-resistant glue such as resin. They are screwed to the sides. Cut the last-named to size, and prepare the two nose-pieces from $\frac{7}{8}$ in. wood. Note that the runners, which are $1\frac{1}{4}$ in. wide, are thinned down at one side only towards the front so that they finish flush with the nose-piece, whereas they overhang the sides. They can be made straight and trimmed flush after fixing.

The simplest plan is to cut out one nose-piece to a fair curve (see Fig. 3) and mark the other from it. The notches are cut with saw and chisel. Note how the end is cut at an angle so that it resists any tendency for the runner to fly out.

In the case of the bottom runner the notch is slightly curved, but do not attempt much curvature because the strain on the holding screws would be too great unless the runner were steamed first. It is better to give a *slight* curve and rely upon a certain amount of shaping after fixing. This necessitates the screws being well countersunk.

At this stage the runners point outwards and are straight. The problem is to fix them to the sides, and a certain amount of improvising is necessary in arranging methods of holding the work. The fixing is greatly simplified if a steaming chamber is available. The wood should be left in for about an hour and bent around pegs or held with clamps. An exact curve is not necessary. If steaming is not possible the bending can be helped by pouring a kettle of boiling water over the wood beforehand. In both cases no glue must be applied over the damp wood. The simplest way is to steam (or damp), screw the runners to the nose-piece and side, and leave to dry. The whole is then taken to pieces, glued, and assembled afresh.

Assembling. Various methods can be used. One is to screw both runners to the nose-piece and fix the side to the lower one. The top one will lie loosely across the side, probably as in Fig. 4 (it depends on the degree of bending already given). Put a block beneath the nose and fix two cramps to hold the lower runner to the bench as

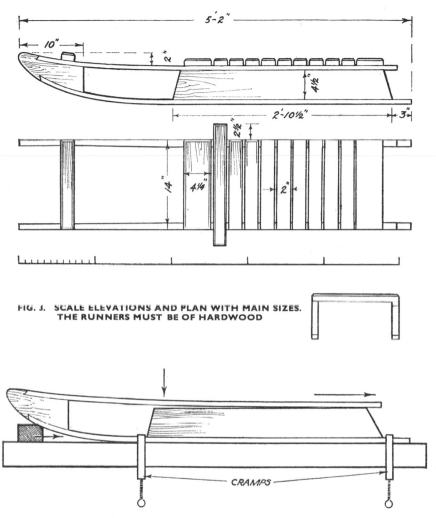

FIG. 3. SCALE ELEVATIONS AND PLAN WITH MAIN SIZES.
THE RUNNERS MUST BE OF HARDWOOD

FIG. 4. HOW THE RUNNERS AND SIDES ARE ASSEMBLED

shown. It is then a matter of adjustment, pushing the block inwards and cramping down the top runner until the degree of rise is correct. The latter is not critical, but both sides must be alike. It may be necessary to pull the top runner outwards as shown by the arrow. When correct the fixing screws can be driven in.

The seat slats can now be fixed. They should be chamfered

around the top edges, and the screws should be well countersunk. Note that the second slat from the front projects so as to form a foot rest for the rear passenger (see Fig. 2). The front and rear slats are wider than the others, and if these have two screws each there is no risk of the whole working out of truth.

If metal runners are used the fixing screws must be countersunk. They should extend up to the nose and be bent around to the top edge. A thickness of about $\frac{1}{16}$ in. is suitable. Brass is free from rusting but is expensive. Iron is cheaper, but needs to be wiped dry after use and given a wipe over with oil.

CUTTING LIST

	Long ft. in.	Wide in.	Thick in.
2 Runners	4 10	$1\frac{3}{8}$	$\frac{3}{4}$
2 Runners	5 1	$1\frac{3}{8}$	$\frac{3}{4}$
2 Nose-pieces	10$\frac{1}{2}$	$5\frac{1}{2}$	$\frac{7}{8}$
2 Sides	2 11$\frac{1}{2}$	$4\frac{3}{4}$	$\frac{7}{8}$
2 Slats	1 2$\frac{1}{2}$	$4\frac{1}{2}$	$\frac{7}{8}$
9 Slats	1 2$\frac{1}{2}$	$2\frac{1}{4}$	$\frac{7}{8}$
1 Slat	1 7$\frac{1}{2}$	$2\frac{1}{4}$	$\frac{7}{8}$

CLOCK FACE FOR THE YOUNGSTERS

THIS INVARIABLY GIVES children a great deal of fun as well as being instructive. The figures are painted on, but if you doubt your skill to make a nice job of them you can use transfers, or you can draw little circles around the figures of a large almanack and cut out and gum these to the face.

Exact sizes are not important. As a general guide that shown in Fig. 1 measures 8 in. by 8 in., but it might easily be an inch more or less. It depends upon the material available. If possible use plywood but it is not essential. A quite good plan is to draw out the face on white cardboard and stick this as a whole to the wood.

The face. Fix down the cardboard with two drawing pins and with compasses put in the various circles. The large band in which the figures appear can be painted blue, red, or any other colour. If figures from a calendar are being cut out these should be pasted on after painting. In the case of transfers these are best applied after the surface has been varnished.

To mark out the hour divisions a 60 degree set-square gives the simplest method. All twelve can be marked with it. For the

FIG. I. USEFUL TEACHING TOY.   FIG. 2. SIDE VIEW

minute divisions mark off between each hour with dividers. If nursery rhyme transfers are available these can be applied at the corners as shown.

Hands. These are best fretted out of thin wood or metal, or even stiff cardboard can be used. The length can be to suit the dial. It is advisable to paint them black. To enable them to remain in any position in which they are placed either a spring washer or a small spring can be used. Procure a rivet long enough to pass through all the thicknesses and drill holes in the dial and hands. Thread on the hands, putting washers between each and at both ends of the rivet. Pass on the spring washer or spring, and burr over the back end of the rivet. A little adjustment will probably be needed to give the required amount of tension.

Strut. This is a plain piece of thin wood hinged at the top as shown in Fig. 2. To prevent it from opening too far a piece of cord can be attached, being tied to screw eyes in strut and dial.

THE EVER-POPULAR ROCKING HORSE

THIS FORM OF rocking horse with stationary stand has largely superseded the older type with curved rockers. It is more suitable for indoor use in that there is no liability for it to gradually work along the floor and into the wall to the detriment of the wallpaper, and there is no danger of its toppling right over.

By building up the body in the form of a box and fretting out head

FIG. I. A TOY WHICH ALWAYS APPEALS TO CHILDREN
Apart from the fun a child gets from rocking on the horse, its bright colours and realistic appearance always have a great attraction

and legs in $1\frac{1}{4}$ in. wood, a quite realistic effect is produced. The body is wide enough to be comfortable to sit on, and the $1\frac{1}{4}$ in. thickness for the limbs enables a certain amount of modelling to be done. It is immaterial whether the horse or stand is made first.

Stand. Prepare four uprights to finish 9 in. by 3 in. by 1 in. and screw them to the top bar (2 ft. 8 in. by 2 in. by 1 in.) so that each pair is 15 in. apart. Fit a similar bottom bar (2 ft. 11 in. long) as in Fig. 2. Note that the ends of both are shaped. Two bars are halved across at the bottom (Fig. 2, right), these finishing 8 in. by 1 in. by 1 in. Note the shaped ends. It is advisable to round over all sharp corners.

The whole thing is mounted bodily upon a base consisting of a main member 3 ft. by 6 in. by 1 in., with two cross-pieces halved and screwed to it finishing 1 ft. 6 in. by 6 in. by 1 in. It is screwed up to the stand from beneath. Once again note the shaped ends. The addition of the top completes the stand. It is 2 ft. 9 in. by 3½ in. by 1 in. and is screwed down. The screws can be recessed and the holes plugged with dowels.

Horse. Make up a box consisting of top, bottom, and two sides. Before putting together cut the halvings in the sides to take the legs.

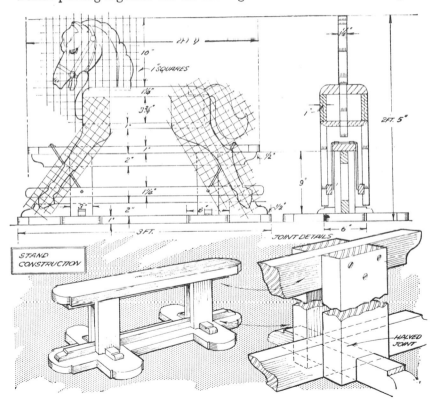

FIG. 2. FRONT AND END ELEVATIONS, AND DETAILS SHOWING HOW STAND IS MADE

The bottom will also have to be notched, but this is best done after it has been fixed to the sides. The front and back have to be filled in with blocks of wood, but this should not be done until after the legs have been added because the last named are fixed with screws put in from the inside (Fig. 3).

The shape of legs and head appears in Fig. 2 set out in 1 in. squares. It is simple to mark out the shape since it can be plotted in graph fashion. First fit the top of the legs to the halvings in the body, cut the joints, and saw the outline. Clean up with spokeshave and file, and round over the corners and edges, finishing off with glasspaper. Glue the joints and screw on the legs. If the screws are entered at a slight angle there should be no difficulty about using the screwdriver.

Quite a lot of shaping can be given to the head, especially at neck and mane. The eyes and ears can also be carved in to give a realistic appearance. The bridle is better added later in the form of actual leather straps, though it could be carved in and painted. Glue the whole thing in the slot cut to receive it in the top, and drive a couple of screws upwards. The tail is treated similarly, though if preferred an old hair brush could be inserted in a hole bored to receive it. When all is satisfactory the front and back of the body can be glued and nailed in.

Pivoting. To enable the horse to rock two rails are fitted between

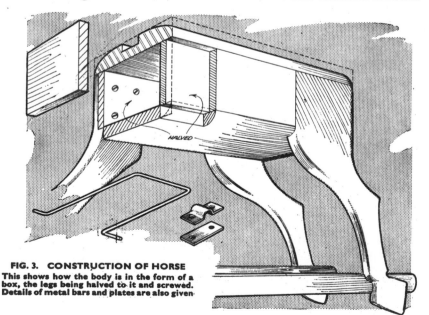

FIG. 3. CONSTRUCTION OF HORSE
This shows how the body is in the form of a box, the legs being halved to it and screwed. Details of metal bars and plates are also given.

the legs in the positions shown in Fig. 2. The legs are slightly recessed to receive them. Holes are bored in them to receive the ends of the cranked metal bars (Figs. 2 and 3). Either $\frac{1}{4}$ in. or $\frac{3}{8}$ in. iron rod can be used for the metal bars. It should be made red hot locally to enable the bends to be made. The ends entering the rails can have washers passed over them and be riveted, or they can be tapped and have nuts screwed on. Where the rods pass over the top of the stand they are held by metal plates as in Fig. 3.

Finishing. The best finish for the horse is oil paint. A good plan is to do all the painting in flat colours, putting in all details and varying the colours where necessary. When thoroughly dry this is followed by a coat of oil varnish. The saddle can be padded out and covered with burlap over which leather is stretched.

CUTTING LIST

		Long		Wide	Thick
		ft.	in.	in.	in.
Horse					
2 Body sides	.. ..	1	6	$3\frac{3}{4}$	1
1 Body top	.. ..	1	6	7	$1\frac{1}{4}$
1 Body bottom	.. ..	1	6	7	1
2 Body ends	.. ..		5	$3\frac{3}{4}$	1
1 Head	.. ..	1	$2\frac{1}{2}$	$11\frac{1}{2}$	$1\frac{1}{4}$
1 Tail	.. ..		10	6	1
4 Legs	.. ..	1	$7\frac{1}{2}$	7	1
2 Rails	.. ..	2	10	$1\frac{1}{4}$	1
Stand					
4 Uprights	.. ..		9	3	1
1 Rail	.. ..	2	8	2	1
1 Rail	.. ..	2	11	2	1
2 Cross pieces	.. ..		8	1	1
1 Top	.. ..	2	9	$3\frac{1}{2}$	1
1 Base	.. ..	3	0	6	1
2 Base pieces	.. ..	1	6	6	1

Sizes are net, so trimming allowance should be added.

DOLL'S CRADLE

A WELCOME PRESENT to any little girl and her doll! It will take a small doll, which can be "rocked to sleep." The construction is very simple, as it consists of two ends, cut to size and shape, as shown on the end elevation drawing in Fig. 2, out of $\frac{1}{2}$ in. ply. The two side frames, top and bottom rails (A, Fig. 2), should be laid side by side, and from this position you can mark off on all four the centres for drilling the dowel holes. Drill the holes to a depth of $\frac{1}{4}$ in., cut the dowels to length, and assemble them into the frames. Screw the ends to the assembled frames, and next screw the bottom to the underside of the lower rail, which will complete the making.

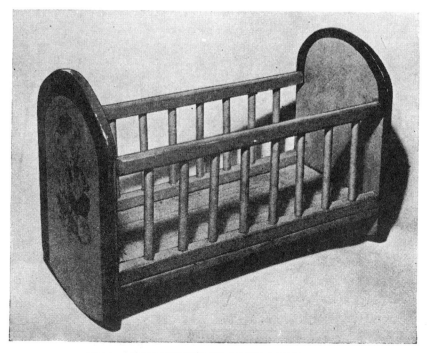

FIG. 1. LOOKS DELIGHTFUL WHEN GAILY PAINTED

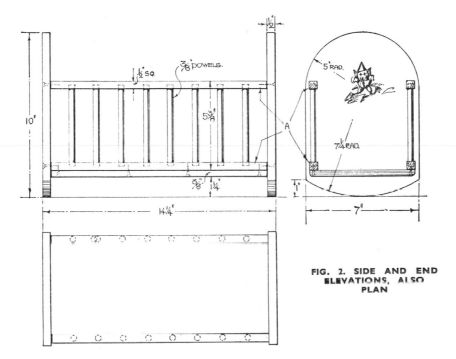

FIG. 2. SIDE AND END ELEVATIONS, ALSO PLAN

Finish in any gay coloured enamel, and add a nursery transfer to the centre of end panels if required.

Notes on painting toys are given on page 153. It is worth taking special care with the finishing as the success of a toy largely depends upon this.

CUTTING LIST

	Long ft. in.	Wide in.	Thick in.
2 Ends	$10\frac{1}{2}$	$7\frac{1}{4}$	$\frac{1}{2}$ ply
4 Rails	1 $1\frac{3}{4}$	$\frac{3}{4}$	$\frac{1}{2}$
1 Bottom board	1 $1\frac{3}{4}$	7	$\frac{3}{8}$ ply
16 Dowels	$4\frac{7}{8}$	$\frac{3}{8}$ dia.	

Allowances have been made to lengths and widths: thicknesses are net.

ENGINE AND TENDER

ENGINES OF ALL kinds are always popular with boys, but one on which a kiddy can actually ride has a particular appeal. That shown in Fig. 1 has proved a great success. It is of reasonably realistic appearance, and has withstood several years of really hard wear and tear. One point to note is that all sharp edges and corners should be rounded over.

The sizes of the parts in Fig. 2 are those of the actual engine shown in Fig. 1. Although arrived at chiefly in accordance with what seemed good design, they were to an extent influenced by the material

FIG. 1. A TOY ON WHICH THE YOUNGSTER CAN RIDE
Well made, it will give years of service

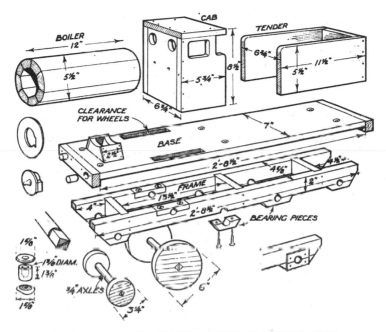

FIG. 2.   MAIN PARTS AND HOW THEY ARE PUT TOGETHER

that happened to be available.   Readers can therefore adapt them to suit whatever wood they may have by them.

One or two points may be noted at the outset.   The wheels are cut from solid wood and are permanently fixed to axles of $\frac{3}{4}$ in. dowel. These revolve in holes cut in the main framework, bearing pieces being provided to enable them to be fitted and removed if required. The boiler is built up cooper fashion, it having been found that a solid one was too heavy.   An alternative would be to cut discs of wood and bend thin plywood around them.

Framework.   This consists of two side pieces joined by three cross-pieces fitting in notches.   Glue and nail the whole together, dovetailing the nails to give maximum grip.

The small wheels are fitted level with the bottom edge, and bearing pieces are fitted to contain them.   Screw on these pieces and bore the holes, inserting the point of the bit exactly on the joint.   Bore in from each side, then allow the bit to pass through to the far side to make sure that they are in alignment.   Mark the position of each bearing so that there is no difficulty about replacing them.

In the case of the driving wheels, these are fitted at the top as shown in Fig. 2. Here again the holes are bored level with the joint which is $\frac{5}{8}$ in. down from the edge. To prevent the wheels from scraping against the framework, little pieces of $\frac{1}{16}$ in. wood are glued and nailed at the outside as shown in Fig. 2. Prepare each pair in a single piece, cut the hole and fix level with the hole in the frame. You can then cut along the joint with a knife, thus enabling the bearing piece to be removed.

Wheels. Mark out with compasses, and cut with the bow saw, cleaning up with the spokeshave. Cut a square at the centre of each to take the square which will be formed at each axle end (Fig. 2). Note that the shoulders cut when these squares are made should allow generous clearance outside the frames.

To mark the shoulders, wrap a piece of thin card around the axle and draw a pencil around this. Make four saw cuts and ease away the waste with the chisel. Pass the wheels over the ends and wedge as shown. Note that the wedges are at right angles with the grain so that there is no risk of splitting the wood. Candle wax can be used to lubricate the bearings, but this should not be applied until after the toy has been painted.

Base. Trim the main board to length (exactly equal to the frame) and screw it to the latter. Mark the clearance for the driving wheels and the slots. When fixing the ends, place the nails so that they clear the buffer holes. The last-named are $\frac{3}{4}$ in. in diameter. Nail the end pieces to the base only, not the frame.

The saddle consists of two pieces of $\frac{1}{2}$ in. wood cut at the top to the curve of the boiler, and joined by two pieces of $\frac{3}{16}$ in. wood. Put together, level the joints, and fix with a few nails driven in askew. Later it is held by a screw passing through the base from beneath into the boiler.

Boiler. This consists of eight pieces put together cooper fashion. The simplest way is to plane all eight pieces to the same width, then bevel all the edges to the correct angle ($67\frac{1}{2}$ degrees) using an adjustable bevel. Glue them together in sets of two each, let the glue set, and put these together to form two complete halves. Fix these together and glue up finally.

Fit in two ends, shaping them to an octagonal shape to fit against the flat sides of the pieces. There should be a 2 in. hole cut in the front end, but fit it first and mark the centre so that the circle of the boiler can be struck out at both ends. Plane to shape and rub down with glasspaper. Fit a disc at the front, and make a door of two pieces glued together to form a rebate. Note the flat right-hand side to enable a hinge to be fitted.

The funnel consists of three pieces glued together. The lower disc is shaped to fit over the boiler, and a hole is bored about half-way down the dowel. A screw driven down fixes it to the boiler.

Cab. Cut the front and bore the holes for the windows. The sides are shaped and glued and nailed to it.

Tender. This is simply three pieces glued and nailed together. The lower edges should be glued, and the whole cramped down to the base. Nails can then be driven upwards through base.

Fix the boiler with a screw through the saddle, and fix the cab to the end with two screws. Cramp down to the base and nail upwards. Doors can be hinged to the back of the cab to open inwards.

CUTTING LIST

	Long ft. in.	Wide in.	Thick in.
Frame			
2 Pieces ..	2 9	$2\frac{1}{8}$	$\frac{3}{4}$
3 Pieces ..	$3\frac{3}{4}$	$2\frac{1}{8}$	$\frac{3}{4}$
10 Bearings ..	$3\frac{1}{4}$	$\frac{3}{4}$	$\frac{3}{4}$
Wheels			
8 wheels ..	$3\frac{1}{2}$	$3\frac{1}{2}$	$\frac{3}{4}$
2 Wheels ..	$6\frac{1}{4}$	$6\frac{1}{4}$	$\frac{3}{4}$
5 Axles ..	$6\frac{1}{2}$	$\frac{3}{4}$ dowel	
Base			
1 Base ..	2 9	$7\frac{1}{2}$	$\frac{3}{4}$
2 Ends ..	$7\frac{1}{4}$	$1\frac{1}{8}$	$\frac{3}{4}$
4 Buffers ..	$1\frac{1}{4}$	$\frac{3}{4}$ dowel	
2 Saddle pieces ..	$3\frac{3}{4}$	$1\frac{7}{8}$	$\frac{1}{2}$
2 Saddle pieces ..	$2\frac{3}{4}$	$1\frac{7}{8}$	$\frac{3}{16}$
Boiler			
8 pieces ..	1 $0\frac{1}{2}$	$2\frac{1}{2}$	$\frac{3}{4}$
2 Ends ..	$4\frac{1}{4}$	$4\frac{1}{4}$	$\frac{3}{4}$
1 Disc ..	5	5	$\frac{3}{16}$
1 Door piece ..	2	2	$\frac{1}{8}$
1 Door piece ..	$2\frac{1}{2}$	$2\frac{1}{2}$	$\frac{3}{16}$
1 Funnel ..	$1\frac{1}{2}$	$1\frac{3}{8}$ diam.	
1 Funnel rim ..	$1\frac{1}{4}$	$1\frac{1}{4}$	$\frac{1}{8}$
1 Funnel base ..	$1\frac{3}{4}$	$1\frac{1}{4}$	$\frac{3}{8}$
Cab			
2 Sides ..	$8\frac{1}{4}$	6	$\frac{5}{8}$
1 Front ..	$8\frac{1}{4}$	$5\frac{3}{4}$	$\frac{5}{8}$
1 Top ..	6	7	$\frac{5}{8}$
Tender			
2 Sides ..	$11\frac{3}{4}$	$5\frac{3}{4}$	$\frac{3}{4}$
1 Back ..	$5\frac{1}{2}$	$5\frac{1}{4}$	$\frac{3}{4}$
2 Doors ..	6	$2\frac{1}{4}$	$\frac{3}{4}$

Allowances have been made in lengths and widths; thicknesses are net.

SWING, SEE-SAW, AND CLIMBING LADDER

IF SPACE ONLY a few yards square can be reserved and fitted up in the garden for the use of the children it will result in their lasting contentment while adding considerably to their health. A suitable fitting, taking but a few hours to build at the cost of as many shillings, is shown at Fig. 1. The space occupied need not be greater than about three yards by four, and the fitting comprises a swing, adjustable see-saw, and a climbing ladder. With such a choice the children are not likely soon to tire, and all help to their physical development.

Sizes. While the dimensions may be adapted to conform with any requirements, it is suggested that the swing should be 8 ft. high,

FIG. I.   CHILD'S GARDEN FITMENT: SWING, CLIMBING LADDER, AND ADJUSTABLE SEE-SAW

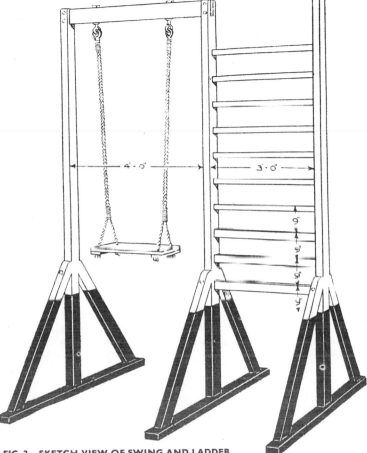

FIG. 2. SKETCH VIEW OF SWING AND LADDER

but some consideration should be given to the ages of the children when deciding on the height of the climbing ladder.   That shown has ten rungs with a total height of 7 ft. 6 in., but for very small kiddies it may be advisable to omit a few at the top at first and add them as they grow older.   It will be noticed that the see-saw rests on the lower rungs of the ladder, and by moving it up or down it may be adjusted to suit children of various ages.   Pine could be used for all the framing, although some may prefer hardwood for the first three rungs of the ladder.

Uprights.   Figs. 2 and 4 show details of three uprights framed to

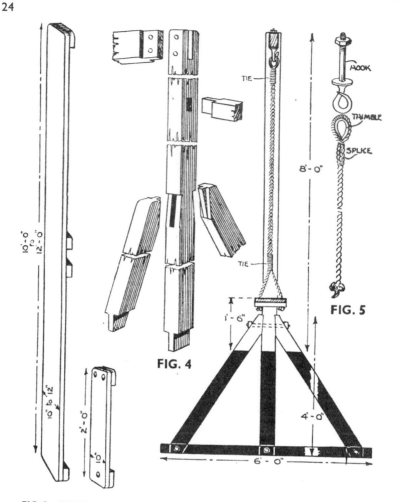

**FIG. 3. BOARD FOR SEE-SAW AND SEAT.   FIG. 4. DETAIL OF JOINTS.
FIG. 5. SWING FIXING. ALSO ELEVATION OF MAIN UPRIGHT**

bearers, stayed with braces, and joined by the swing headpiece and the ladder rungs.   The uprights are 11 ft. long, tenoned into bearers 6 ft. long, the latter being placed on the flat.   Braces are tenoned through the bearers and notched and stub-tenoned to the uprights. All joints through the bearers could be fixed with bolts, and long bolts are used to fix the braces on each side of the uprights.   Full details of the joints are given in Fig. 4.   It takes about an 86 ft. run of $4\frac{1}{2}$ in. by 3 in. pine or fir for the main framing.

Head-piece.   The swing head-piece is bridle-jointed to the top ends of the uprights, and should be fixed with $\frac{5}{16}$ in. bolts to enable it to be easily removed should occasion demand. All the ladder rungs should be 3 ft. 6 in. long, the three bottom ones could be of hardwood 3 in. wide by $1\frac{1}{4}$ in. thick, and those above of pine 2 in. wide by 1 in. thick. Most of the rungs need only be tenoned $1\frac{1}{2}$ in. into the uprights, but one at the top and another at the bottom could be tenoned right through and pinned.

Trenches for the bearers and uprights must be prepared in the ground, the bearers being sunk to a depth of 3 ft., and the wood treated with tar, thick paint, or patent preservative. The two uprights carrying the swing should be placed in the trenches and the head-piece fitted and bolted. A plumb-line could be used for truing up as the frames are firmly embedded. The remaining ladder upright is then placed in its trench, and the rungs fitted and fixed.

Ropes. The best means of attaching the swing ropes to the head-piece is with strong hooks, having screws to carry through the head-piece and nuts for fixing. It is necessary, however, to see that the hooks themselves are well formed, and that their points are turned around sufficiently to give safe attachment. Metal thimbles such as those used in ship and boat work should be provided for fitting the swing ropes. There may be a single rope at each side, with the thimble spliced in, as shown at Fig. 5, or a double rope may be used and the thimble tied in without a splice. A rope of the latter kind could be brought down to within about 1 ft. from the seat where it is tied again, and the free ends passed through two holes in the seat board and knotted. The latter (see Fig. 3) should be 2 ft. long by 10 in. wide, strengthened with battens at the ends.

See-saw. The board of the see-saw may be from 10 ft. to 12 ft. long by from 10 in. to 12 in. wide. A thickness of $1\frac{1}{4}$ in. is essential, and it should be strengthened by screwing battens across the ends as shown at Fig. 3. Two battens are also screwed across the middle, with a space of about 2 in. between, their object being to keep the board from slipping on the rungs when in use.

In making a fairly large structure such as this the question of timber has to be considered. In country districts where felling is taking place it may be possible to obtain off-cuts and other oddments which could be used.

As in all other similar toys all edges and covers should be well rounded over with the plane and then thoroughly glasspapered. In the case of second-hand timber look particularly for splits and cracks as these easily cause splinters. Remember to punch in all nails and fill in the holes with plastic wood or putty. Level down with the chisel when it has set.

ZOOLOGICAL FURNITURE

ANIMALS APPEAL TO all young children, and to present them with a chair or a piece of furniture embodying an animal's shape will give great joy, especially when it is different from "grown-up" furniture. The animals selected are such as lend themselves to a bold and simple outline treatment. All of them have an outstanding feature—such as the elephant with its trunk which can be understood by the child without a lot of fussy detail being needed. At the same time, it is easy for the amateur artist to undertake the painted details. Although there is no necessity for artistic talent, a good pencil brush is essential. The construction is simple and the designs can be quickly made, enamelled, and upholstered with padded seats.

Constructional methods for the two chairs are the same, and having obtained the required number of sides in $\frac{1}{2}$ in. plywood, sand them on both sides. On one side draw two-inch squares lightly in pencil using them as a guide to drawing in the animal outline (Figs. 2, 3, and 7). The outline can then be cut out with a fretsaw or bowsaw and used as a template for the matching side, thus ensuring complete

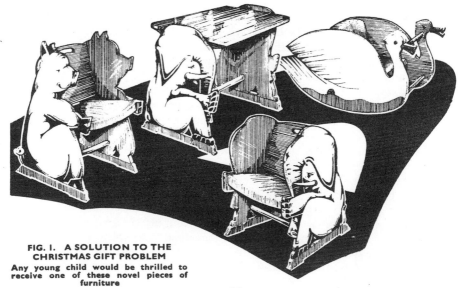

FIG. I.   A SOLUTION TO THE CHRISTMAS GIFT PROBLEM
Any young child would be thrilled to receive one of these novel pieces of furniture

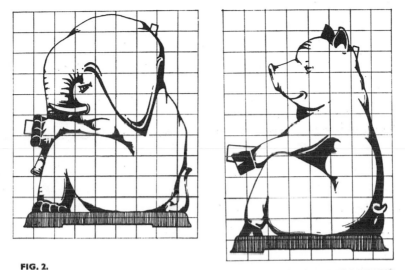

FIG. 2.
THE OUTLINE FOR THE ELEPHANT   FIG. 3.   THE OUTLINE FOR THE PIG
Each square in both diagrams represents 2 inches, and the shape can be enlarged by plotting
in graph fashion on full size squares

accuracy.   Glasspaper the sawn edges smooth, at the same time removing the sharp edges and corners all round the sides.

Now cut and shape the fillets (A and B) in Figs. 4 and 6, and mark off the relative positions as indicated, remembering they are right- and left-handed.   They must be in complete alignment as otherwise the chair will be distorted when assembled.

Next, carefully mark the position for boring the mortise holes for the under-rail (D, Fig. 4), which is a $\frac{3}{4}$ in. diameter hole.   This under-rail is a 1 in. diameter dowel papered smooth and reduced at each end to give a tenon $\frac{3}{4}$ in. in diameter   (see E, Fig. 4).   This should be a tight fit, and is through-tenoned and wedged from outside.   Before finally fixing this under-rail, screw into position the seat and back fillets from the outside.   The screw holes can either be pelleted or filled with wood-filler and papered smooth.   They will not show when painted.

The backboard is $\frac{1}{2}$ in. thick plywood cut to size and shape, with a hand-hole cut through at the top (F, Fig. 4).   Glasspaper the sawn edges and screw into position from the outside of the fillets.   Do likewise with the seat-board, a plan of which is shown in Fig. 4. Before fixing this should be padded with a piece of 1 in. thick latex or plastic foam fixed to it with a suitable adhesive (H, Fig. 4); it is then covered with a plastic fabric which can be wiped over with a damp

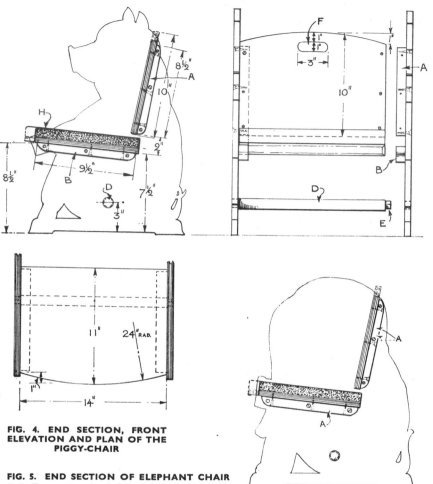

FIG. 4. END SECTION, FRONT ELEVATION AND PLAN OF THE PIGGY-CHAIR

FIG. 5. END SECTION OF ELEPHANT CHAIR
A similar construction is followed for all the chairs

cloth when soiled. The fabric should be pulled to the underside of the seat-board and tacked into position. However, it should be cut to size and tacked into position temporarily and removed when enamelling is being done to avoid spoiling it.

Now that the chair is assembled and the seat removed, apply one coat of undercoat enamel, followed by the finishing background enamel, completing by "lining-up" the details. A suggested colour-scheme for the elephant would be to enamel it in a mid-grey, using a dark grey or black for the "lining-up" and colouring the tusks a

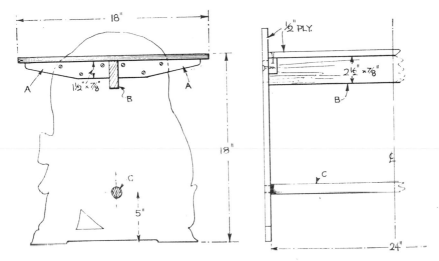

FIG. 6. END SECTION AND HALF-FRONT ELEVATION OF ELEPHANT TABLE

white or ivory colour. A flesh-colour background would be appropriate for the pig, "lining-up" with a brown. In both cases the base should be green. Having screwed the seat finally into position, the chair is complete.

The table. Fig. 6 shows a playtable incorporating the elephant design for the sides, the outline of which is identical with the one described above. Assuming the sides have been cut, the general construction consists of a centre-rail (B, Fig. 6), and an under-stretcher (C) which is again a 1 in. dowel reduced at each end to make a $\frac{3}{4}$ in. tenon. Both rails are through-tenoned and wedged

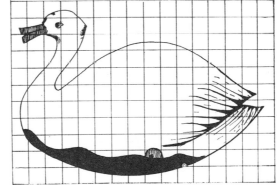

FIG. 7. OUTLINE OF ROCKING DUCK
Each square represents 2 in.

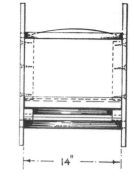

FIG. 8. SIDE AND FRONT ELEVATIONS OF ROCKING DUCK

from the outside. The top is $\frac{1}{2}$ in. plywood, supported by a centre-rail and brackets (A, Fig. 6), which are screwed to the inside of the ends. The top, in turn, is screwed down on to the brackets, and a half-plan of this is shown in Fig. 9.

The enamelling procedure is the same as for the chairs, and as an added attraction, the table-top could be lined with a plastic material.

FIG. 9.

CUTTING LIST

				Long ft.	Long in.	Wide in.	Thick in.
Chairs							
2 Sides	..	..	..	1	10	18	$\frac{1}{2}$ ply
1 Seat	..	..	..	1	3	11	$\frac{1}{2}$ ply
1 Back	..	..	..	1	3	11	$\frac{1}{2}$ ply
4 Fillets	..	..	..		10	1	$\frac{7}{8}$
1 Stretcher rail	..	..	..	1	4	1 dia. dowel	
Table							
2 Sides	..	..	..	1	10	18	$\frac{1}{2}$ ply
1 Top	..	..	..	2	1	19	$\frac{1}{2}$ ply
1 Top rail	..	..	..	2	2	$2\frac{3}{4}$	$\frac{7}{8}$
4 Brackets	..	..	..		9	$1\frac{3}{4}$	$\frac{7}{8}$
1 Stretcher rail	..	..	..	2	2	1 dia. dowel	
Rocking chair							
2 Sides	..	..	..	2	7	21	$\frac{1}{2}$ ply
1 Back	..	..	..	1	3	11	$\frac{1}{2}$ ply
1 Seat	..	..	..	1	3	11	$\frac{1}{2}$ ply
4 Fillets	..	..	..		10	1	$\frac{7}{8}$
1 Footboard	..	..	..	1	4	$3\frac{1}{4}$	$\frac{7}{8}$
1 Hand-rail	..	..	..	1	4	1 dia. dowel	

Allowances have been made to lengths and widths; thicknesses are net.

Rocking duck. Fig. 7 illustrates a rocking chair with a duck motif for the sides, the bases of which form a rocker.

In general, the construction follows that described for the chairs. Mark out one of the side-outlines using the 2 in. square method, and use the cut-out as a template for the matching side. Having cleaned them up, mark off and screw into position the seat and back supporting fillets (A, Fig. 8). The seat should slope down towards the back as this helps to seat the child well back into the chair, which is, of course, necessary when the chair is rocking forwards.

Footrest (B, Fig. 8), and hand-rail (C) are both through-tenoned and wedged from the outside, C also acting to stiffen the whole structure. The latter is again a length of 1 in. dowel, cleaned up and with the ends reduced to form a $\frac{3}{4}$ in. diameter tenon. Both the seat and back should be padded, with either latex or plastic foam (D, Fig. 8), which is fixed with an adhesive. Place the seat and back temporarily into position and having assured yourself that the assembly is accurate, remove them before starting enamelling. A suitable colour-scheme for the duck would be a background of off-white with the feathers lined-in in black. Use a deep orange for the beak and a blue (to represent water) for the base.

MINIATURE LAWN MOWER

A NOVELTY TOY with all the appearance of a real mower, it will no doubt appeal to the "boy" of the family, and can be used indoors without fear of the carpet pile being cut off. It operates with a satisfying "clicking". It is quite simple in its construction; the materials required are beech and plywood. The whole thing is painted in the colours suggested.

Start by making the side plates (Fig. 3) out of $\frac{1}{2}$ in. thick plywood, and cut them in the shape shown. Each square in the diagram represents 1 inch and having cut one side out it can be used as a template for the other. After cutting, glasspaper off, smoothing the edges well to prevent splintering. Mark out and drill the holes for the $\frac{5}{8}$ in. connecting dowels, noting that they should be drilled to give a tight fit. Next, the centre hole should be drilled for the driving shaft, which also is a $\frac{5}{8}$ in. dowel, but in this case, it should be an easy fit to allow the driving shaft to rotate easily and smoothly. Drill hole for the roller pin and the screw securing the handle. The final assembly cannot be undertaken until the blade attachment, clicking cog wheel and roller are made.

The first part to fix will be the blade attachment and then the clicking wheels, set at the clearances shown in Fig. 4, on the driving shaft. Now saw to length the three $\frac{5}{8}$ in. dowels, which should be a tight fit in to

FIG. I. THE COMPLETED MOWER

32

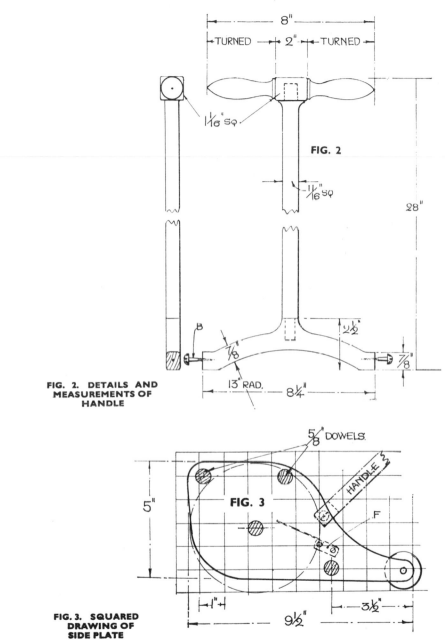

8"

TURNED 2" TURNED

FIG. 2

1 1/16" SQ.

1 1/16" SQ.

28"

FIG. 2. DETAILS AND MEASUREMENTS OF HANDLE

B

7/8"

2 1/2"

7/8"

13" RAD.

8 1/4"

5 5/8" DOWELS

FIG. 3

HANDLE

F

5"

1"

3 1/2"

9 1/2"

FIG. 3. SQUARED DRAWING OF SIDE PLATE

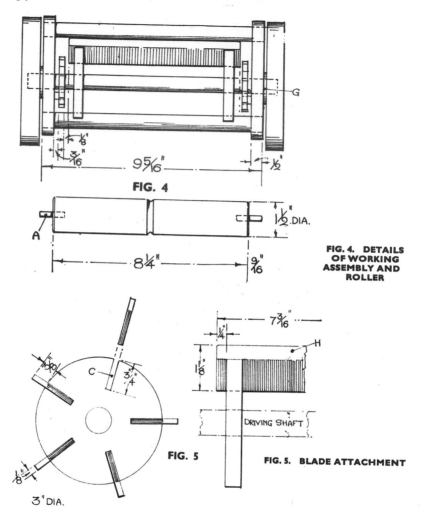

FIG. 4

FIG. 4. DETAILS
OF WORKING
ASSEMBLY AND
ROLLER

FIG. 5

FIG. 5. BLADE ATTACHMENT

the side plates. Take care when assembling to see that the side plates
are parallel and the fixing holes in alignment. It would be an
advantage to wedge the dowels.

Blade attachment. The blade attachment (Fig. 5) consists of
two discs, each 3 in. in diameter and comprising five blades. The
discs are from $\frac{3}{8}$ in. plywood with five slots cut $\frac{3}{4}$ in. deep as at C
(Fig. 5), the slots being a tight fit for the blades, which are $1\frac{1}{8}$ in. by
$\frac{1}{8}$ in. plywood. Set the blades so that there is a $\frac{1}{4}$ in. overhang and

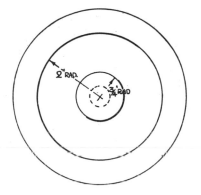

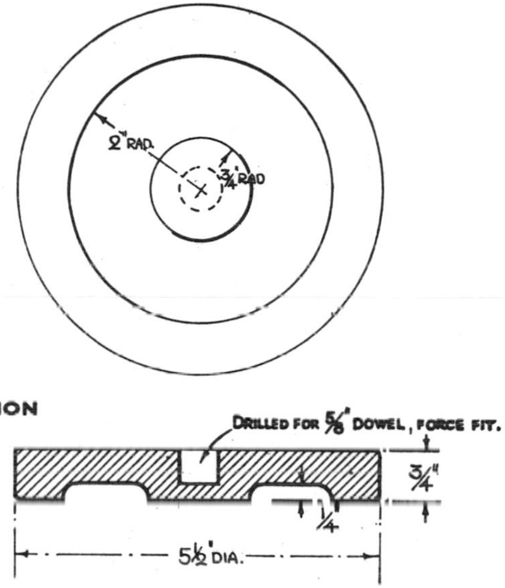

FIG. 6. ELEVATION AND SECTION OF DRIVING WHEEL

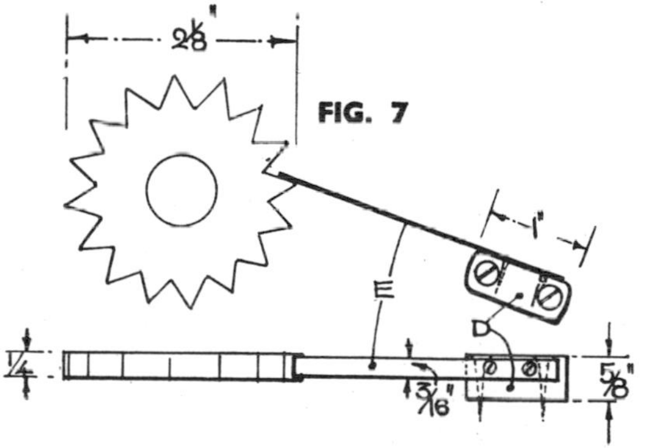

DRILLED FOR 5/8" DOWEL, FORCE FIT.

3/4"

1/4

5½" DIA.

2⅛"

FIG. 7

E

D

1/4

3/16"

5/8"

FIG. 7. THE "CLICKER" MECHANISM

glue them. The assembly can then be driven on to the driving shaft.

The click-wheel is of course only needed to give the familiar running sound (Fig. 7). It is 2⅛ in. diameter and out of ¼ in. thick plywood, and has sixteen teeth. To create the clicking sound, procure two pieces of spring metal about 3 in. long and, say, $\frac{3}{16}$ in. wide. These should be screwed to a small block of wood (D, Fig. 7), which is in turn screwed to the inside of the side plates. The block must be located in such a position that the spring just engages the cogs to produce the "click" (F, Fig. 3).

Handle. The beech handle (Fig. 2) is in three parts, namely the hand grip, the shaft, and the yoke. The hand-grip is turned at both ends leaving a square in the centre into which the shaft is tenoned. The shaft is shaped to the sizes as shown, and is, in turn, tenoned into the yoke. The yoke having been marked out and cut to shape is held in position by round-headed screws (B, Fig. 2), which are screwed through the sides.

The sizes of the driving wheel are given in Fig. 6, and it is face-turned on the outside face to the section shown. Counterbore it on the inside to accept the driving shaft with a tight fit. Before assembly a metal washer is placed between the side plates and the driving wheel (G, Fig. 4). Again, beech is used for the driving wheel.

The handle as far as the yoke is clear polished or varnished, the yoke being painted red, and the roller is beech, clear polished. The blades and the two wheels holding them are red, except the edge of the blade (the unshaded part as at H, Fig. 5), which is finished with aluminium paint. Aluminium paint is also used for the dowels and cog wheel, and the sideplates are green on both sides. The face of the centre boss on the driving wheel is green, and the sunken part red. The rim is green, and the edge is either aluminium-painted, or a piece of rubber could be fixed on as an imitation tyre.

CUTTING LIST

	Long ft.	in.	Wide in.	Thick in.
1 Hand grip..		$8\frac{1}{2}$	—	$1\frac{1}{16}$ sq.
1 Shaft	2	$2\frac{1}{2}$	$1\frac{3}{16}$	$1\frac{1}{16}$
1 Yoke		9	$2\frac{3}{4}$	$\frac{11}{16}$
2 Driving wheels		6	$5\frac{3}{4}$	$\frac{3}{4}$
1 Roller		$8\frac{3}{4}$	—	$1\frac{1}{2}$ sq.
3 Dowels		10	—	$\frac{5}{8}$ dia.
1 Driving shaft dowel..	1	0	—	$\frac{5}{8}$ dia.
2 Side-plates		10	$5\frac{1}{4}$	$\frac{1}{2}$ ply
2 Blade discs		$3\frac{1}{2}$	$3\frac{1}{4}$	$\frac{3}{8}$ ply
5 Blades		$8\frac{1}{8}$	$1\frac{3}{4}$	$\frac{1}{8}$ ply
2 Cog-wheels		$2\frac{5}{8}$	$2\frac{3}{8}$	$\frac{1}{4}$ ply

Also required: 2 pieces spring steel, 2 washers, $2\frac{3}{8}$ dia. metal pins for roller. Allowances have been made in lengths and widths: thicknesses are net.

TOY SCALES

FOR THE TWIN uprights (A) take two lengths of $\frac{3}{8}$ in. wood 8 in. long. Width at base may be $1\frac{1}{4}$ in., tapering to 1 in. at top. Cut tenons to enter the base. These uprights are placed $\frac{3}{8}$ in. apart and are supported at foot by the piece (B), $2\frac{1}{2}$ in. by $1\frac{1}{4}$ in., and $\frac{3}{8}$ in. thick, which is glued to them.

Base. The base (C), to be firm, should be $\frac{1}{2}$ in., squared up to 10 in. by 4 in., and finished with chamfered edges. Toes are optional; if used they may be 1 in. square, cut from any scrap of thin wood.

The bar (D), of $\frac{1}{4}$ in. wood, is $7\frac{1}{2}$ in. long by $\frac{1}{2}$ in. wide. Mark the centre and drill a fine hole. By passing a wire through this hole the balance may be tested and any necessary adjustment made. To fit the bar, drill through the uprights about $\frac{3}{4}$ in. from top and

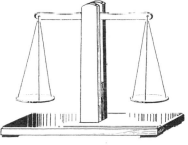

FIG. I. COMPLETED TOY

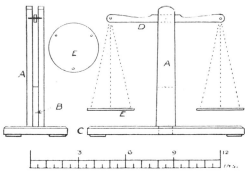

FIG. 2. ELEVATIONS WITH SCALE

pass in wire $1\frac{1}{8}$ in. long and $\frac{1}{16}$ in. diameter. The balance bar (D) is slipped on to this wire with a thin metal washer on each side. On the uprights stop up the holes drilled for the wire.

Discs. Discs (E) may be 3 in. in diameter. Use $\frac{1}{8}$ in. plywood, painting the edges, and suspend with stout cotton thread. Any adjustment in the balance can be made by gluing pieces of card to the underside of the lighter disc.

NOAH'S ARK AND ANIMALS

A NOAH'S ARK is a popular traditional toy which never seems to lose its appeal to youngsters, and it tends to hold their interest over a period of time.   This one is very simple, as shown in Fig. 1, the base or hull being in solid wood, and the rest in plywood.   On pages 44–48 are full-size outlines of animals which can be traced and cut out in plywood.   Projections are left at the bottom of each foot, these being glued into a base which is cut to receive them.   The base can also be of plywood, cut to a suitable size for each animal.   Ply $\frac{1}{4}$ in. thick should be suitable in most cases, but larger animals, such as the elephant, would be better with a somewhat thicker base.

The dimensions given in Fig. 2 make quite a large ark, and if these are varied, the general proportions should be retained.   The best policy is first to make as many animals as are required, then see how

FIG. I.   FOR THE YOUNGER CHILDREN
If preferred only the animals could be made up
See pages 44/48

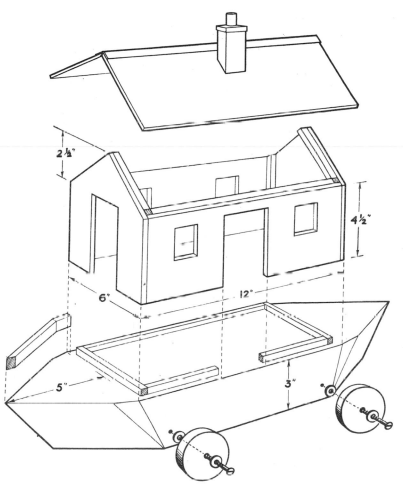

FIG. 2. SIZES AND CONSTRUCTION OF THE ARK

much space they will demand when packed away. If desired, additional space can be allowed in planning the ark, so that further animals can be made later on.

Animals. The general principle of building up the animal shapes is shown in Fig. 3, three layers of plywood being used. The centre layer is shaped to incorporate body and head only (with tail, where necessary), and the two outer layers include legs, but are minus head and tail. Shoulders are chamfered off on the outer layers, as shown,

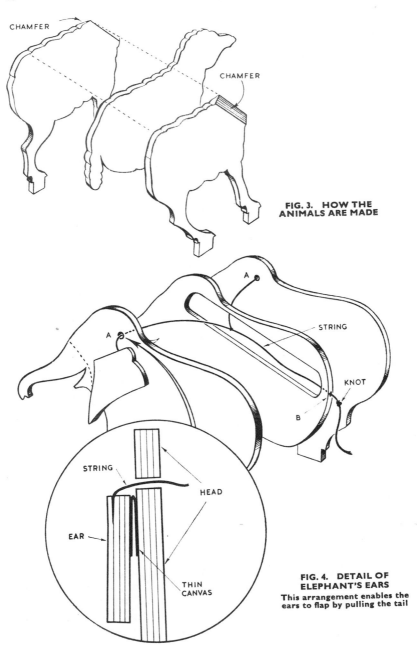

CHAMFER

CHAMFER

**FIG. 3. HOW THE
ANIMALS ARE MADE**

A

A

STRING

KNOT

B

STRING

HEAD

EAR

THIN
CANVAS

**FIG. 4. DETAIL OF
ELEPHANT'S EARS**
This arrangement enables the
ears to flap by pulling the tail

to avoid any ugly corners. This method gives the animals something approaching natural proportions, and the thickness of plywood can be varied to suit the size of the animal. For the largest animals, $\frac{1}{4}$ in. ply should be used for each layer, but the smallest ones need only $\frac{1}{8}$ in. Edges of the plywood can be rounded off with glasspaper if required, again giving a more natural effect, but where very thin legs are involved, it is best not to round these to any extent, or they will be weakened.

On pages 44–48 the shapes of the layers are indicated where necessary by dotted lines. Legs on the rear outer layer are shown by thin dotted lines, and the centre layer of the body by thick dotted lines. The whole principle can of course be varied as required, and animals such as the duck, pelican, penguin, rabbit, and seal are best cut from a single layer of $\frac{1}{4}$ in. ply, both sides being painted identically. For the duck and penguin $\frac{1}{8}$ in. ply could be used. Noah himself is also designed as a single layer of $\frac{1}{4}$ in. ply.

A further variation is to include the head on all three layers, as in Fig. 4, although in this particular case it would be better to chamfer off the two outer layers so that they finish where the trunk joins the face (see dotted line) thus leaving the trunk itself and the mouth on the centre layer only. Similarly, in the case of the lion, it is a good idea to include his mane and ears in the outer layers, but leave the rest of his face on the centre layer only.

Flapping ears for elephant. The arrangement shown for the elephant in Fig. 4 adds a novel touch in the form of flapping ears. The latter are cut separately from plywood and hinged to the head by gluing on strips of thin canvas (see sectional sketch, Fig. 4, inset). The outer layer of the plywood ear is prised up locally and the string securely glued inside for some distance. The string runs through a hole (A) in the outer head, through a slot cut in the centre ply layer as far as the rear end, where it goes through a hole (B) to emerge as the tail of the elephant. Inside the head the string branches into two to provide the same arrangement for both ears. Once assembled a knot is tied just outside at the rear, so that the knot comes up against the hole when the ears lie flush against the head. Thus, by pulling the tail, the ears are made to flap. As shown in the sectional sketch, the ears will only lift satisfactorily if the string is fixed at their outer top edge, thus providing leverage.

Building the ark. If a single piece of wood is not available for the base of the ark, two or three layers can be glued together to make up the thickness of 3 in. The sides are left upright except at both ends, which are planed to a slope as shown in Fig. 2. Although two distinct facets are shown at each end, the corners left can be rounded if required, or the whole merged into a continuous curve. In any case, the sharp bottom corners left at either end of the base should be well rounded off and the top corners slightly rounded.

The superstructure is of $\frac{1}{4}$ in. plywood, with fillets glued into internal corners to hold the walls together. The plywood is also pinned to the fillets from outside for extra strength. The same principle is followed for fixing the superstructure to the deck. A deck rail can be added at both ends, as shown.

Roof. This is in two halves, hinged together at the ridge by a strip of canvas glued on as shown in Fig. 6. The roof could be made of hardboard, but, if a really strong job is required, use $\frac{1}{4}$ in. ply, and hinge the two halves with small brass butts, which can be covered with the canvas strip.

The chimney stack is simply a piece of solid wood glued on and screwed from inside the roof. Make sure the screws go into the stack at an angle, which will afford a better hold in end-grain. The side of the roof with the stack on it is fixed to the walls by fillets, but the other side is left free to be lifted as required. Position the stack so that the free half can rest against it when open.

Attractive windows can be made up as separate units, in the form of thin sheets of clear perspex. Sash bars and outside frame can be added to this in the form of coloured perspex strips stuck to the clear perspex sheet with acetone. The complete window unit is fixed over the window aperture of the wall and shutters added on either side.

Ramp. A useful feature is a hinged flap on the side door, which can be let down as a ramp for the animals to leave the ark. Fig. 5 shows the principle, a recess being made in the side of the ark base the same width as the doorway. The flap is in two halves, hinged together at Y, and the whole is hinged to the ark at X. A stop (E) is provided for the flap to close against, and a swivel catch can be fixed at the top of the doorway to hold the flap up when closed. Fig. 5 (B) shows the flap when let down.

Wheels. If a lathe is available, the simplest way of making the wheels is to turn a cylinder from which the wheels can afterwards be sawn. Make them about $\frac{7}{8}$ in. thick and about $2\frac{3}{4}$ in. to 3 in. in diameter.

Alternatively, they can be cut out with a coping saw and smoothed off afterwards with rasp and glasspaper. The wheels turn on screws driven into the side of the ark, washers being placed on either side of each wheel.

Painting. Start with a good foundation of flat white paint before finishing in the required colours. This applies to the animals as well, since plywood will absorb the initial coat to a large extent.

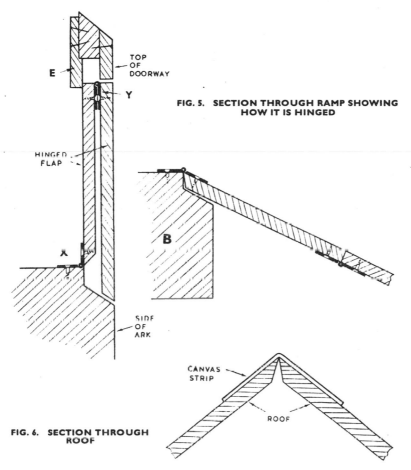

TOP
OF
DOORWAY

E

Y

FIG. 5. SECTION THROUGH RAMP SHOWING
HOW IT IS HINGED

HINGED
FLAP

B

X

SIDE
OF
ARK

CANVAS
STRIP

ROOF

FIG. 6. SECTION THROUGH
ROOF

Markings shown on the animals on the patterns can be copied on to
the plywood in varying colours. For the ark itself a dark colour
might be used for the base, with lighter wheels. Walls of the superstructure would look well in white, and the roof in red, the effect of
tiles being added in black lines. Green window shutters will provide
an attractive finish.

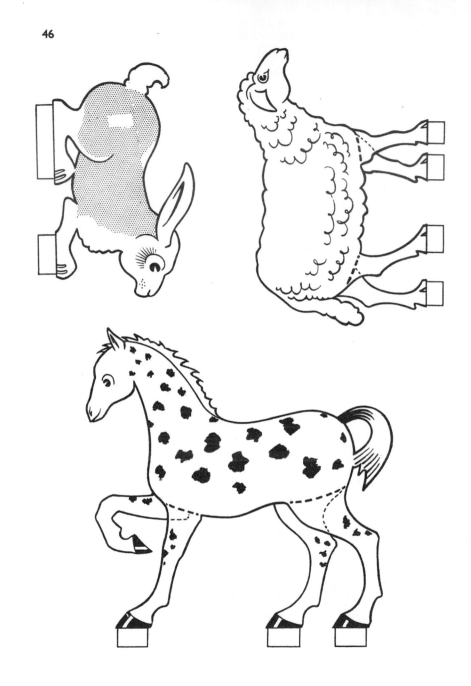

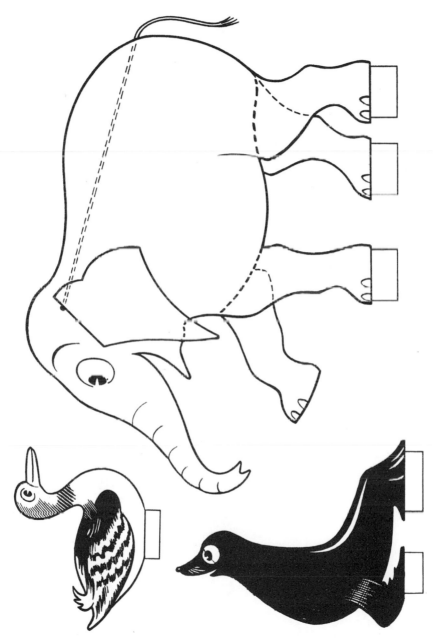

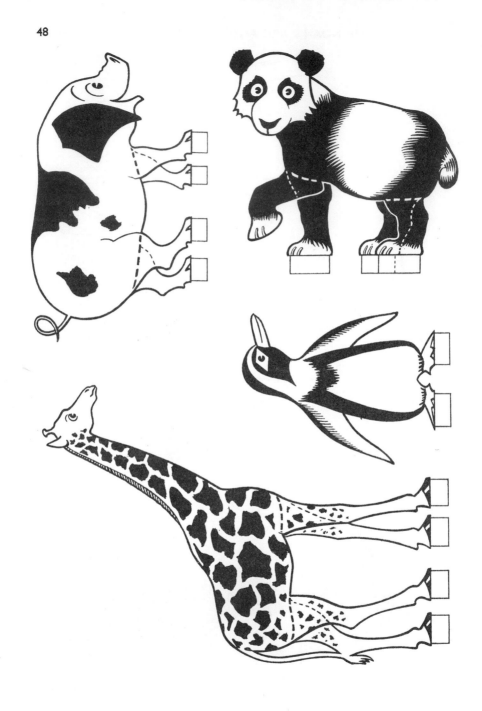

SHIPS ON WHEELS OR TO FLOAT

SHIPS ALWAYS APPEAL to boys, and here are some simple ones that will delight the younger children.

Battleship. For this you can use any stout piece of timber. The exact size doesn't matter a bit. Draw in a centre line, and mark the curve at the bow by bending a thin lath of wood and pencilling in. The curve at the stern can be drawn either with compasses or with some rounded object such as a bowl or large tea cup. Mark both top and bottom. To cut the shape the simplest plan is to use the ordinary handsaw, making a straight cut as close as possible to the line. It may be possible to make two or more cuts. Afterwards a broad chisel is used to pare down the corners to the shape. The ordinary smoothing plane can be used to finish off, this being followed by glasspaper.

The deck houses, decks, and so on are glued and nailed on. Funnel and mast should fit in holes and be glued in. Dowel rods, old broom handle, or any rounded pieces of wood can be used. Gun turrets are held with a round-head screw so that they are free to pivot. Wheels can be added or the ship left as it is to float. Grey is the most suitable colour.

Cargo boats and liners. These can be made from any scraps up to 5 or 6 in. long. Keep the deck fittings quite simple with just

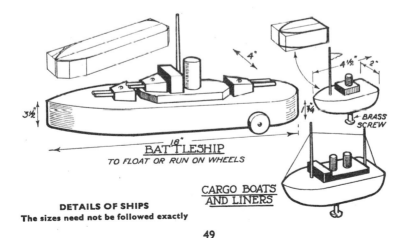

BATTLESHIP
TO FLOAT OR RUN ON WHEELS

BRASS SCREW

CARGO BOATS AND LINERS

DETAILS OF SHIPS
The sizes need not be followed exactly

49

the essentials. The hull is shaped in plan first and then the lower corners taken off. One or more brass screws according to the size gives stability to the ship when floating. Paint the hull white or black, the decks a buff colour, and the sides of the upper decks a brown. Funnels can be copied from those of real ships. It will be found an advantage to paint the parts before fixing together as it saves over-running with the brush.

TUMBLING CLOWN

THIS FUNNY LITTLE clown tumbles from rung to rung without breaking his neck!—and creates a lot of fun and laughter. The making is so simple that it needs hardly any explanation once you have read the drawings. Getting the sizes correct is the main object. The colouring of the clown is indicated on the colour chart in Fig. 2.

The material required is two lengths for ladder sides, 24 in. by $\frac{7}{16}$ in. square, a base board 4 in. square and finished $\frac{3}{4}$ in. thick, and a piece of wood for the clown, sizes being $3\frac{7}{16}$ in. by $1\frac{1}{4}$ in. by $\frac{11}{16}$ in. thick.

It adds to the fun to have a second clown, as when one is half-way down the ladder the second one could be started.

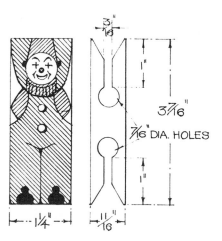

FIG. I. DETAILS OF THE CLOWN
A key to the colours is given in Fig. 2

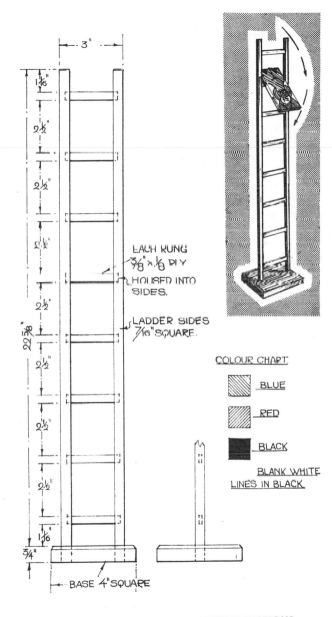

- 3"

1 1/16"

2 1/2"

2 1/2"

2 1/2"

EACH RUNG
3/8" x 1/8" DIY
HOUSED INTO
SIDES.

LADDER SIDES
7/16" SQUARE.

2 1/2"

22 5/8"

2 1/2"

2 1/2"

2 1/2"

1 1/16"

3/4"

← BASE 4" SQUARE

COLOUR CHART

BLUE

RED

BLACK

BLANK WHITE
LINES IN BLACK

FIG. 2.   PERSPECTIVE VIEW, WITH ELEVATIONS
The above chart can be used in conjunction with Fig. I

A SAND MOTOR

THIS SIMPLY BUILT toy is popular owing to its dual capacity. It is a complete toy for the child, providing all the joys of the sand pit on a smaller scale; and is a source of power for the elder child to attach to and animate small models.

Construction is simple. It can be made of plywood and hard-board, and consists of the body or carcase into which the rotor is fitted. The axle upon which the rotor revolves is formed into a small crank at one end and from this point the movement is obtained to work models. Above the rotor is a hopper into which dry silver sand is loaded to trickle through the central orifice into the buckets formed in the rotor, thus operating the motor. A tray which can be made to any desired dimension contains the complete unit, so keeping the toy clean and suitable for a table game. To manipulate the sand, a small scoop can be made from plywood offcuts.

The rotor. Mark out and cut two circles of plywood about $\frac{1}{8}$ in. thick, the centres being clearly marked and bored out a tight fit on

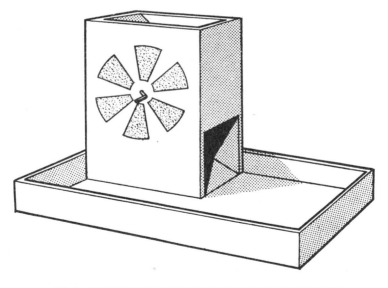

FIG. I. MECHANICAL TOY TO GIVE ENDLESS AMUSEMENT

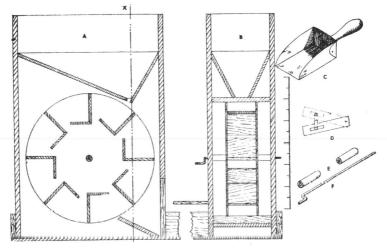

FIG. 2. SECTIONAL SIDE AND END VIEWS, AND SMALL DETAILS

the axle. This part should be made accurately to ensure that it revolves truly when mounted. A good plan is to thread the circles upon the axle, press both together, and mark around the outer edges eight equal divisions on the inner faces of the circles. From the marks made on the edges draw radial lines, these being used to locate the buckets when gluing up later.

Now cut off and prepare the material for the buckets. This may be of $\frac{1}{8}$ in. ply or hardboard. See that the length is accurate as otherwise a fair joint cannot be made when erecting the rotor. Glue up as a sub-assembly each back and bottom, keeping the ends flush and level. Put aside to dry. Assemble the buckets upon one circle of the rotor sides. Lay this upon a flat surface, inside face upwards, and well glue each bucket with the bottom of each bucket lying exactly upon the radial lines drawn on the circle and flush to the outer edge. When this has set, glue the end joints of the buckets standing uppermost and place the remaining side in position, taking care that the edges are flush and true.

If this work has been carried out carefully the rotor should spin true when the axle is pushed into position. Should it wobble a little, however, do not attempt to alter it as a certain amount of latitude has been allowed in the hopper feed to accommodate this possibility.

The carcase or body. Plywood is the best material for this part. Cut out and square up, and, placing the two sides together, locate and drill a hole that will allow the axle to rotate freely. An added attraction can be given by cutting perforations in the sides as shown in Fig. 1 and painting the faces of the rotor.

The better method of fixing the frame is with small wood-screws bored through the faces of the sides and secured to the ends. The back is dry screwed only to facilitate removal of the rotor if required at any time. Having prepared these parts it is necessary to prepare the axle (F) and spacing collets (E) before assembling. For the axle procure a straight piece of $\frac{1}{8}$ in. iron wire and fashion one end into a crank having about $\frac{1}{4}$ in. throw. This is not critical but if over-large may probably cause the motor to work sluggishly when models are attached. If any difficulty is met in forming this axle, make the wire red hot, when it will bend easily with a pair of pliers. The collets can be made from a piece of $\frac{1}{2}$ in. dowel, a hole being bored in the centre to accept the axle. The length of these is arranged so that the rotor has a little end play. The rotor must revolve freely.

To assemble the body glue and screw the front to the ends, push the axle through the bearing hole and place a collet in position. A touch of *Durafix* will secure this to the axle. Now push the rotor on the axle, again securing with a touch of adhesive, and finally fix the remaining collet. The back can be placed in position, and, all being correct, the rotor should revolve centrally and truly in the frame.

Interior. The position of the plywood sides forming the hopper are shown in Fig. 2. There is nothing particular about them other than a little neat fitting. They only need securing with glue. The outlet should not be too large or the sand will run too quickly.

The deflector board at the base can be closely fitted and glued and, if desired, a small shelf may be fitted to form a base to any model being operated (see side section). To obtain movement for a model various methods can be used but generally, if a slot is used, it is possible to obtain either vertical or horizontal movements, either being governed by the direction of the slot in the model, the model being pivoted always in the line of direction of the slot. This is shown at D.

SUBURBAN DOLL'S HOUSE

THE FRONT OPENS in two parts to the left of the doorway disclosing four rooms, hall and staircase. The roof is fixed on permanently, but a flap is arranged at the back to give access to a loft in which batteries can be kept in the event of the rooms being electrified. The staircase is set at 45 degrees, thus simplifying the tread arrangement, since the wood has only to be planed at 45 degrees and cross-cut. This brings the foot rather close up to the front door, but this does not matter a lot in a toy. If it is started a little farther back the flight will be steeper and the angle of the tread blocks must be altered accordingly.

FIG. I. AN EVER-POPULAR PRESENT FOR A GIRL
Finished in strong colours this makes a most attractive toy. It is 2 ft. 6 in. wide across the front, 1 ft. 3 in. deep, and 2 ft. 6 in. high over all

56

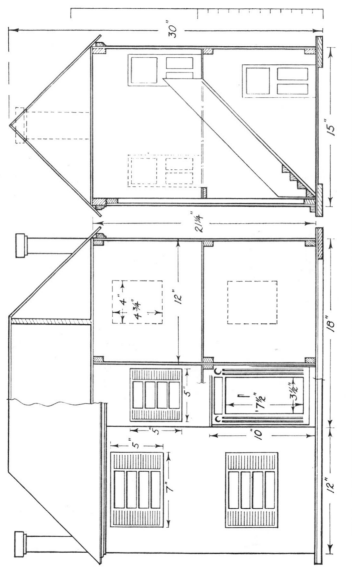

FIG. 2. FRONT ELEVATION SHOWN IN PART SECTION, AND SECTIONAL VIEW THROUGH THE SIDE

The construction is similar whatever covering material is used and consists of light frames of 1 in. by $\frac{1}{2}$ in. stuff halved together and covered with plywood, plastic board, or hardboard. The choice affects the main sizes to an extent since the thickness varies. Plastic board, for instance, will probably be $\frac{1}{16}$ in. thick, whilst plywood and hardboard will be thicker.

Make up the four frames for the two side and two inner walls, halving the joints as in Fig. 3. Cut out the covering material and mark the door positions in the inner walls. Glue and nail them to the frames, leaving the outer frames until later. Prepare another frame for the back and fix to it the end frames with the glue and nails. It is necessary to cut the inner frames to fit over the rails. Incidentally, if plastic board is used, the surface should be well rubbed with coarse glasspaper where it is to be glued. Otherwise there will be poor adhesion. Nails pass through thin plastic board quite easily.

Floors. Prepare the upper floor in three pieces, and cut the well for the stairs. Fix them down on to the mid-rails of the frames and add rails at the front at the underside to prevent sagging. Finally, fix the back covering and, having trimmed the edges, add the sides. The bottom is in a single piece mounted on a mitred framework, and is screwed on from beneath. Note that it has a greater projection at the front than at the sides owing to the fronts having to be added.

As the fronts have clearly to be beneath the overhang of the roof it is necessary to fix a rail at the top along the front, the width being equal to, or a little more than, the downward projection of the roof. It is fixed straight along the front as shown in Fig. 4, and the top covering glued and nailed on afterwards. A finish is given by adding a moulding all round as shown in Fig. 2.

Roofs. To provide a fixing for these, triangular pieces are fixed to the top as in Fig. 4. The angle is 45 degrees, and they are set in from the ends by an amount equal to half the back-to-front distance. The simplest way of obtaining the shape of the roof pieces is to lay a sheet of stiff brown paper in position and fold it so that it aligns with the apex corners. Cut the covering full to shape, trim as necessary, and fix down with glue and nails. A strip of gummed tape along the ridges gives a neat finish and strengthens the whole. The hole in the back roof for the flap can be omitted if desired. Otherwise the flap can be hinged with a piece of leather or tape glued along.

Chimney stacks are plain blocks with capping pieces. The strongest fixing is by screwing from beneath, and if this is done it is necessary to fix them before the ends roofs are secured.

Fronts. For these cut out the covering material in two parts and fit them to the house. Mark in the window and door positions (see

58

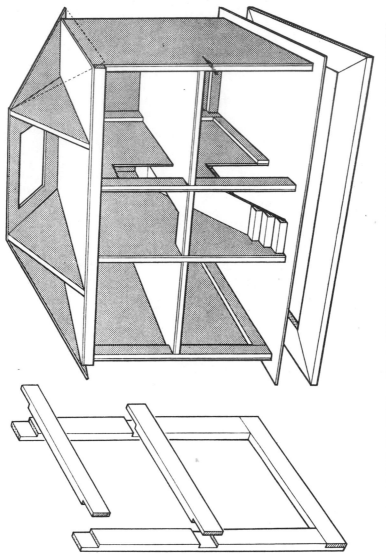

FIG. 3. HOW FRAMES ARE MADE.   FIG. 4. FRONTS AND PART ROOF REMOVED TO SHOW CONSTRUCTION

dotted lines in Fig. 2) and fret out. Each window frame with its shutters is in a single piece glued on. Note that the window opening size in the frame is less than that in the fronts by ¼ in. all round, so providing a rebate in which glass or Perspex can be fitted. The door framework is also in a single piece, fretted out and glued on. The door itself can be hinged with a strip of tape inside.

Fitting and finishing. Interior fittings are best left to individual requirements. Doors, mantelpieces, and other fittings can be made up and added as a whole. Fig. 4 shows how the strip for the staircase is fixed and the blocks glued on. A solid balustrade is the simplest to arrange.

Flat oil colour paints can be used for finishing, or you can use the special doll's house brick, tile, or stone papers made for the purpose. If covering paper is used it is advisable to defer fixing the window and door frames until afterwards.

CUTTING LIST

	Long ft.	Long in.	Wide in.	Thick in.
Covering material				
4 Walls	1	9½	14½	—
1 Back	2	6½	21½	—
1 Front	1	8¾	12¼	—
1 Front	1	8¾	18¼	—
1 Top	2	6½	15½	—
1 Bottom	2	8½	17½	—
2 Floors	1	0	14½	—
1 Floor		6½	14½	—
4 Window Frames		7¼	5¼	—
1 Window Frame		5¼	5¼	—
1 Door Frame		10¼	6	—
2 Roofs	2	9	12½	—
2 Roofs	1	6	12½	—

If in plastic, board thickness is about $\frac{1}{16}$ in. Hardboard varies from ⅛ in. upwards. Same thing applies to plywood. The above lengths and widths are affected within a little by the thickness of the covering material

	Long ft.	Long in.	Wide in.	Thick in.
2 Floor Battens	2	8½	3	½
2 Rails	2	6½	1½	½
2 Roof Pieces	1	3½	8	½
2 Chimney Stacks		8½	2¾	1½

About 45 ft. battening, 1 in. by ½ in.
Small parts extra. Allowance for trimming has been made.

OF NURSERY TOYS few are more satisfying than the make-believe shop, especially when made to a fair size. If desired, an altogether larger toy could be made, say 3 ft. long by 2 ft. 6 in. to 2 ft. 9 in. high.

Counter. For a useful counter of the size suggested the parts required will be these:

				Long ft.	Long in.	Wide in.	Thick in.
(A)	2 Ends	..	..		6	$4\frac{1}{4}$	$\frac{1}{2}$
(B)	Front	..	..	2	3	6	$\frac{3}{8}$
(C)	Shelf ..	..		2	$2\frac{1}{2}$	$4\frac{1}{4}$	$\frac{3}{8}$
(D)	2 Partitions	..			$4\frac{3}{4}$	$4\frac{1}{4}$	$\frac{1}{2}$
(E)	Top ..	..		2	$3\frac{1}{4}$	$5\frac{1}{4}$	$\frac{1}{4}$

The ends (A) are trenched for the shelf (C) which will be glued in. The front (B) is glued on and additionally held with a few panel pins. It can also be glue-blocked at the corners and under the shelf. The two partitions (D) are housed to the shelf, and the top (E) is glued down and either panel-pinned or blocked; all nail holes should be neatly stopped.

If to be painted, the counter front may be lined to represent panel-

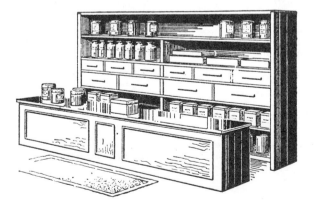

FIG. I.   THE NURSERY SHOP
Size of display case, 27 in. by 18 in.   Size of counter, 27 in. by 6 in. high

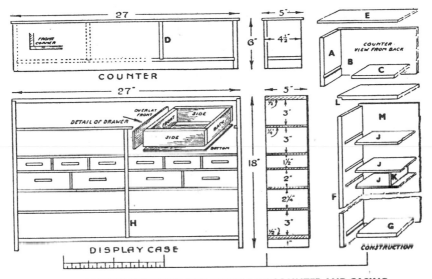

FIG. 2. SCALE ELEVATIONS AND DETAILS OF COUNTER AND CASING

ling; or, if preferred, the panelling may be effected by means of narrow (say, $\frac{1}{4}$ in.) strip detail. A pair of toy scales, with weights, should be procured.

Drawers. These for toy purposes can be made in the simple manner indicated if the worker has facilities for cramping up small glued work. Using $\frac{1}{4}$ in. for fronts and $\frac{3}{16}$ in. for sides and backs, the parts may be glued together. Thin $\frac{1}{16}$ in. plywood will serve for the bottom, also glued on. If all parts have been correctly gauged and are well cramped in the gluing they will stand constant wear. The actual front is, of course, a dummy, and later a thin overlay (either $\frac{1}{16}$ in. fretwood or plywood) is glued over all to hide the joints. Wood handles or knobs will be added.

Display case. This, in detail, may vary slightly as the worker pleases, but it is wise to follow the general dimensions given. The sizes are these:

				Long		Wide	Thick
				ft.	in.	in.	in.
(F)	2 ends	..	..	1	6	$5\frac{1}{8}$	$\frac{1}{2}$
(G)	Bottom shelf		..	2	$3\frac{3}{4}$	$5\frac{5}{8}$	$\frac{1}{2}$
(H)	Partition	..	..	1	$1\frac{1}{4}$	$5\frac{5}{8}$	$\frac{1}{2}$
(J)	5 Shelves	..	..	2	3	$5\frac{5}{8}$	$\frac{1}{4}$
(K)	2 Drawer Divisions	..			$2\frac{1}{2}$	$5\frac{1}{8}$	$\frac{1}{4}$
	2 Drawer Divisions	..			2	$5\frac{5}{8}$	$\frac{1}{4}$
(L)	Top	..	..	2	$3\frac{1}{4}$	$5\frac{5}{8}$	$\frac{3}{8}$
(M)	Back (ply)	..	..	2	$3\frac{1}{4}$	$17\frac{1}{4}$	$\frac{1}{16}$

For the drawer fronts allow one length 26 in. by 2 in. by $\frac{1}{4}$ in. and one length 26 in. by $1\frac{1}{2}$ in. by $\frac{1}{4}$ in.

Lengths given above allow for fitting, but all the thicknesses are net.

As the display case and counter will be painted any wood may be used. For lasting wear, however, it is wise to select a hardwood. Plywood may of course be used for parts which are not prominent "show" wood.

For the ends, bottom shelf and top it is wise to use $\frac{1}{2}$ in. stuff. The bottom shelf (G) is housed to the ends (F), whilst the top (L) is rebated on, glued and pinned. The partition piece (H) should be housed to the bottom shelf and nailed to the upper shelf (J). If drawers are to be introduced, it is well to house in the intermediate shelves (J) to both ends and partition. Shallow grooves should also be run in these shelves for the division pieces (K), the little extra trouble being worth while if the drawers are to run smoothly. The work should be carefully gauged, as it is an advantage (to children at least) if the drawers can be interchangeable.

Many dummies can be made up to resemble packages, tins, bottles, etc. They can be mostly cut out of wood, and when painted look most realistic. A box of artist's oil colours is handy for this.

FOLDING SLIDE FOR THE YOUNGSTERS

IT MUST BE admitted that, like the swing or the see-saw, a make-shift arrangement for a "slide" often gives far more enjoyment to children than a skilfully planned structure. It is the early make-shifts of our own contrivance that most of us look back on with pleasure. The arrangement shown in Fig. 1, however, is a popular one with children.

Length, height, and angle you must determine for yourself, these depending on the age of the child and the space available. The end view (Fig. 2) and side elevation (Fig. 3) will be a guide as to general construction.

Slide. The slide (A) is pivoted at top to the supports (B). The angle or slope is thus determined either by the length of slide or the height of support. A shorter slide (or, alternatively, a higher support) makes the slope steeper. The slide, if about 5 ft. 6 in. long, can be made with two sides (C) of 2 in. by $\frac{7}{8}$ in. stuff, held at intervals by cross bars (D) which may be dovetailed on (Fig. 6) or merely nailed (Fig. 7). For the top a 13 in. wide board of $\frac{1}{2}$ in. plywood may be nailed on (Fig. 4), or, if preferred, a stouter board ($\frac{5}{8}$ in.) may

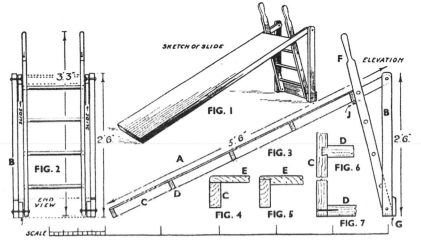

AN OUTDOOR TOY THAT FOLDS AWAY IN A SMALL SPACE

be rebated and nailed on as at Fig. 5. Round all edges and drive all nails well home. As seen in Fig. 1, the plywood board finishes about 9 in. from upper ends of sides (C), this to allow for the step-ladder (F).

Supports. The supports (B) should, for strength, be of 2 in. by 1⅛ in. At the foot they are held by a 3 in. or 4 in. by ⅞ in. board (G) nailed across. They are stoutly bolted to the slide sides (C) as indicated, washers being placed between the parts to prevent friction. The pivoting arrangement permits of the supports being folded against the slide.

The step-ladder (F), made to a width that will work freely between the slide sides, may have shafts of 2 in. by ⅞ in. and rungs of ⅞ in. diameter. The top ends can be shaped as handles. The ladder is pivot-bolted to the supports (B), just clearing the ground, and it may be found desirable to fit small thicknessing pieces (see Fig. 2) to compensate for the thickness of slide side which, of course, comes between the supports and the ladder. The ladder shafts butt against the top cross bar of the slide, which might be fixed slightly on the bevel; and, to keep things steady, it may be wise to fit short iron pins or hardwood dowels (J) to the shafts immediately under the cross bar.

Bear in mind that a folding structure of the kind will be apt to slip, and for this reason it may be well to fit short iron spikes to the foot of each support (B) and also to the ground cross bar of the slide. This, in moments of rough play, will prevent the risk of slipping. The whole should be painted with the exception of the top which should be left in the bare wood.

DUTCH CARPENTER SCARECROW

THIS NOT ONLY serves to scare away birds from the garden, but it is a constant source of amusement to children. The parts required for the carpenter are given full size on these pages, so that all you have to do is to trace them.

It is worth while studying the accompanying diagrams so that you see exactly how the scarer works. To the end of the propeller shaft a piece of wire is fixed, this bent to form a crank. Another piece of wire is bent to a loop at one end and is screwed to the saw. The loop (X) passes over the crank, so that as the latter revolves the saw is moved back and forth, being kept in a horizontal position by the straight part of the wire which passes through a hole in the log. The movement of the saw is imparted to the figure whose body and arms move to and fro.

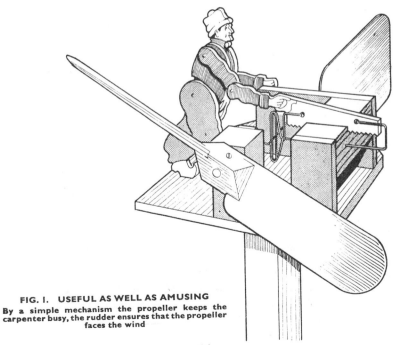

FIG. I. USEFUL AS WELL AS AMUSING
By a simple mechanism the propeller keeps the carpenter busy, the rudder ensures that the propeller faces the wind

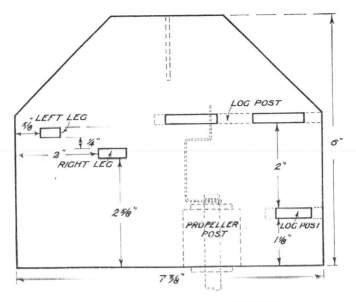

FIG. 2. PLAN OF BASE BOARD WITH SIZES

The figure. On a piece of tracing paper trace round the outline of all the parts given on pages 66–67. Note that two side body pieces are needed. Stick the tracings to ¼ in. wood or plywood, and saw around the outline with a fretsaw. The approximate positions of the pivoting holes can also be marked, but they need not be drilled at this stage because it is an advantage to experiment to find the exact position. Glue the side body pieces to the main body, and, when dry, level the edges with glasspaper.

You can now paint the figure straightway. Oil colours are the most durable. Go over all the parts with a flat colour, and when dry paint in the finished colours, putting in the features, etc., as opposite, but omitting small detail. Follow with a coat of clear oil varnish. An alternative is to use showcard or poster water colours, following with two coats of varnish. These are rather simpler to manage, but the result is not quite so durable. Pay special attention to the edges which show end grain.

To pivot the limbs you can either use screws or bifurcated rivets. In the case of screws the thread is a tight fit in the one part and the shank an easy fit in the other, thus allowing free pivoting. It is advisable to stagger the arms slightly so that the screws miss each other.

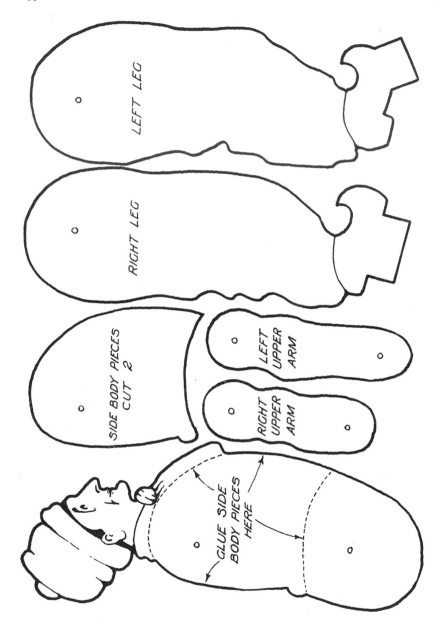

PARTS OF THE FIGURE AND DETAILS IN FULL SIZE

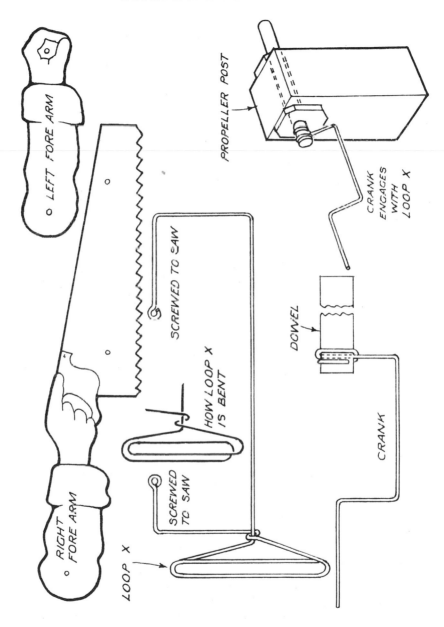

THE OUTLINE OF THE PARTS CAN BE TRACED

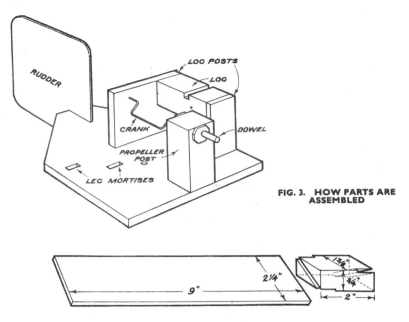

FIG. 3. HOW PARTS ARE ASSEMBLED

FIG. 4. DETAIL OF PROPELLER BLADES AND BOSS

Baseboard. Cut this to the size given in Fig. 2, cutting the leg mortises to take the tenons of the legs. Prepare also the log and its posts as in Fig. 3. They also are tenoned in. The propeller post is bored with a $\frac{1}{2}$ in. hole near the top to take the dowel which forms the shaft, and is fixed with a single screw driven upwards through the base. To ensure the shaft turning easily a little piece of ply is fixed at each side, these having a $\frac{3}{8}$ in. hole bored through them. Thus the shaft, which is a $\frac{3}{8}$ in. dowel, bears only on the plywood.

The full-size drawing shows how the crank is fixed to the dowel. It passes through a small hole, is taken a couple of turns round, and then bent to form the crank. The same illustration also shows the detail of loop X and its extension. The whole thing is formed from a single piece of wire. The ends are screwed to the saw.

Propeller. Fig. 4 gives details of this. The centre boss is a plain block of wood with a centre hole to take the shaft, and slots running diagonally at the ends, these holding the blades. Use $\frac{1}{8}$ in. wood for the last named, rounding the ends and thinning off the edges. Glue up and fix to the shaft with a small screw.

For the rudder use a piece of $\frac{1}{8}$ in. plywood, cutting slots in both it and the baseboard to give a fixing. It then remains only to pivot the baseboard on a post.   The exact balancing centre must be found, and the simplest way is to turn the whole thing upside down and by trial and error find the balancing point.   Bore a hole and pivot on a long screw, using a washer both above and below.

Rub all bearing parts well with candle-grease before putting together.   To assemble, pass the crank through loop X and into the hole in the log post, put the propeller post over the shaft, and fix to the base with the screw.   Add the propeller, and finally·fit on the post.

BRICK TRUCK

PAINTED IN BRIGHT and varied colours these always appeal to youngsters.   Any oddments can be used.

Truck.   As a general guide a length of 9 in. by 6 in. is about right, but the exact sizes are unimportant, except that they should be arranged so that the bricks will make an easy fit.   Cut the opposite sides to the same length and nail them together.   A base of plywood is nailed underneath.   Note that all corners and edges are rounded over.   Fix two square axles beneath by screwing downwards through the bottom, allowing a slight projection at each side.   The wheels are wooden discs pivoted on round-head screws.

Bricks.   These should all be cut to the same size.   Square up the wood in lengths and round over the edges.   A stop fixed to the cutting block enables any number to be cut to the same size.   Round over the remaining edges and all corners.   Finish with varied colours. To avoid the difficulty of handling when the paint is wet stick three pins into one side.   These can then be held whilst painting, and the bricks can be supported upon them whilst drying.   Allow to dry thoroughly before use.

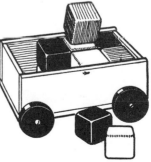

THE BRICKS CAN BE CUT FROM ANY STANDARD SIZE OF TIMBER, AND THE TRUCK MADE TO SUIT

TWO SIMPLE DOLL'S HOUSES

WHEN MAKING EITHER of these houses you have to consider first the materials you have to hand. Plywood is extremely useful, but if you have not enough you will have to fall back upon solid wood, joining pieces in their width and strengthening with cross battens. The sizes can be adapted if a larger or smaller house is more convenient.

Small house. This is a quite simple two-room structure with front opening in a single piece. Cut out the various parts to the sizes given, and if necessary add battens at the inside to strengthen the joints. Windows are best cut out with the fretsaw. Glasses can be added by one of the methods shown in Fig. 7. At A a front frame is glued on to form a rebate. A bead is fitted round at B, whilst at C the framework fits inside, the opening being larger than that in the front itself. Triangular pieces of wood or cardboard hold the glass.

Fig. 3 shows how the house is put together. The floors are nailed between the sides, and the back nailed on. At the front a strip is fixed in front of the top ceiling. The front proper fits beneath this and is thus not liable to foul the projecting roof. The latter is nailed on. Hinge the front to the right, using butts: for the small door a strip of canvas will prove effective.

Special doll's house paper can be obtained for both inside and outside. An alternative, however, is to distemper inside and give a stucco effect on the walls. The latter can be produced with plaster of Paris, dabbing on a fairly stiff mixture with an old stubby brush. When dry it can be distempered a pale buff. The roof can either be painted or

FIG. I. SIMPLE DESIGN,
12 in. by 9 in. by 19 in.
Either cover with doll's house brick paper, or give a good stucco effect with plaster of Paris

70

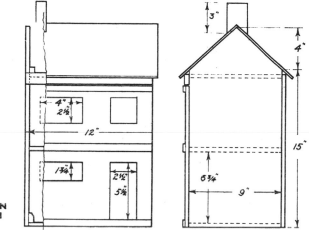

FIG. 2. ELEVATION
AND PLAN WITH
SIZES

strips of wood can be nailed on to overlap rather in the manner of
shingle boards. For the chimney a solid piece of wood can be
prepared with a V cut at the bottom.

Larger house. Fig. 4 shows a completed view of this, and Fig. 5
the construction. There are four rooms, or three rooms and a hall
if one likes to put in a staircase. The front opens in three parts,
two to the right and one to the left. Having cut out the parts first
fix the floors between the side walls, nailing through as shown in
Fig. 5. Slide in the inner walls and skew nail them. The back
wall is nailed on; also the front gable. A simple framework for the
base can be either halved together or fixed at the corners with
wriggled nails. Screw on from beneath.

For the roofs, put the right-hand
parts together first. It runs right
through as in Fig. 6. The sizes can
be taken direct from the house itself,
a slight overhang being allowed.
The same thing largely applies to the
left-hand roof. To obtain the
correct angle where they lie over the
roof already fitted, the best plan is to
cut out a piece of stiff paper or card
as a template and trim the wood to
this. In any case cut the wood
somewhat full to allow for trimming.

IF SIDES ARE JOINTED
ADD BATTENS

FIG. 3. HOUSE CONSTRUCTION
AND FRONT

FIG. 4. LARGER HOUSE, SIZE 19 in. by 12 in. by 24 in.

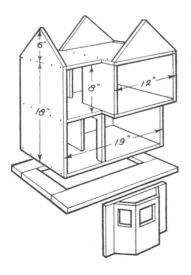

FIG. 5. LARGER HOUSE CONSTRUCTION

When making the fronts fret out the holes for the windows, if necessary gluing and nailing battens at the back.   If this is done upright battens must be fixed at the ends also.   Fit with hinges at the ends, and put a hook and screw eye to hold the fronts. Glasses for the windows can be fixed as in Fig. 7. The bay window is made up complete and fixed to its front as in Fig. 5. Battens to give a half-timbered effect are glued and nailed at the gable, but these should not be added until after the house has been painted.   The same thing applies to window sills and any other similar details.

The reader can use his ingenuity on such fittings as window curtains

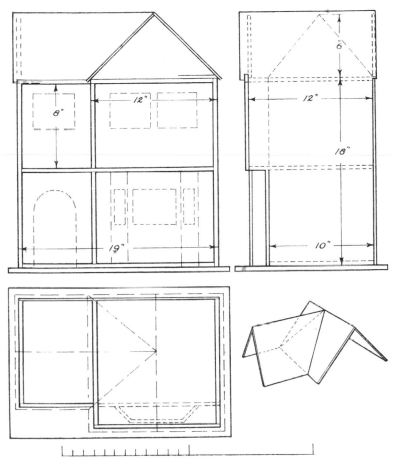

FIG. 6.   FRONT AND SIDE ELEVATIONS AND PLAN OF LARGER HOUSE

—little oddments of material can be pleated and nailed up. Fitments and furniture too can be added.   Fireplaces, dressers, and shelves add greatly to the attractiveness of the house.   If stairs are fitted the best plan is to cut a hole in the first floor to give emergence upstairs, and fix a sloping strip of wood.   On this a series of triangular blocks can be fixed to form the stairs.   A solid side painted to resemble panelling is simpler to make than a rail and bannisters.

Chimneys can be added, solid blocks being cut to fit the angle of the roof.   Dowels can be put in the top to form chimney pots. Inner doors can be plain pieces of wood, painted and hinged with

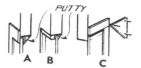

FIG. 7. FIXING WINDOW
GLASS

glued tapes. For the front door strips of thin wood can be glued on.

The inner and outer treatment can be similar to that of the smaller house in Fig. 1. If a stucco effect is not desired the walls can be distempered in any suitable light colour. The base framework usually looks well if painted green to resemble grass.

It will be realised that the sizes and construction given are largely by way of suggestion. Much depends upon the wood available. The best plan is for the reader to sort out the material he has and select pieces most suitable for the various parts. It may be necessary to adapt the dimensions given in Fig. 6.

Incidentally you can give a most realistic effect to the interior by cutting out illustrations of carpets from old catalogues. Many of these have large illustrations in colour, and they look very well. Edgings can be stained or painted.

TOYS ON WHEELS AND STANDS

THERE IS AN almost unlimited variety of toys of this kind that you can make. A glance through a child's picture-book will make many suggestions.

Animals on wheels or stands. For these you can either saw the shape out of a single piece of wood, say $\frac{1}{2}$ in. or $\frac{5}{8}$ in., as in the zebra; or you can use two pieces of $\frac{3}{8}$ in. wood as in the lamb. The advantage of the latter method is that you can show four legs in a realistic form. Plywood, $\frac{1}{4}$ in. or $\frac{3}{8}$ in., has the advantage of being considerably stronger. The shapes can be cut with a coarse fretsaw, and the corners rounded over. Where the feet join the stand, holes to receive them can be cut. The colouring, though founded on nature, should be bold and bright, and have a touch of humour in it. A good plan is to cut out animals from coloured or plain picture books. The latter could be painted. Screws serve as axles for the wheels, which are cut from wood.

Wriggling serpent. This is best made in a single length as shown in the diagram. After the joints have been cut the parts are held together and a hole drilled through. This enables fine nails to be passed through and be riveted beneath. Another plan is to make

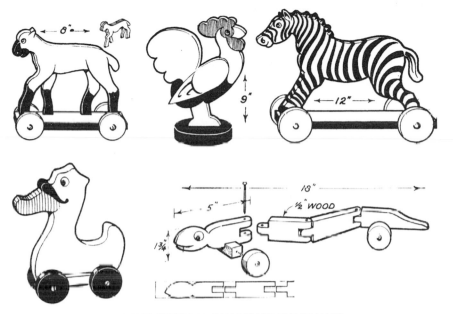

A FEW OF THE ANIMALS THAT CAN BE MADE

the hole in the middle piece an·easy fit and the others tight. This saves riveting.

Windmill. Here you can make a simple box with one end pointed, roof pieces being nailed over here. The sails consists of two little centre blocks $1\frac{1}{2}$ in. or 2 in. long halved together. At both ends of each a slanting cut is made with the saw (make sure that all slope in the same direction) and a piece of either stiff cardboard or thin plywood glued in. The whole revolves upon a brass round-head screw. If the wood of the house is thin a little thicker block can be glued inside to give a bearing for the screw. At the front another block is needed to enable the sails to clear the roof, or alternatively several washers can be used. The sails will revolve freely if the toy is placed in the wind. It could be used to frighten birds in the garden.

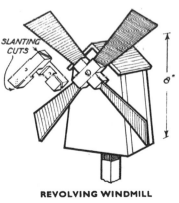

REVOLVING WINDMILL

ANIMAL RIDING TOYS

FOR CHILDREN WHO are lovers of animals and are not afraid of a crocodile or dachshund (on wheels), here is a toy that is completely different. A good softwood such as parana pine is suggested to form

FIG. I. AN UNUSUAL TOY FOR ACTIVE YOUNGSTERS
This can be made in the shape of various animals (see also Fig. 3)

the body and legs. The thickness could be anything up to $1\frac{3}{4}$ in. and depends upon over-all finished length. If this is difficult to obtain, get something as near as possible to this but not less than $\frac{7}{8}$ in. If $\frac{7}{8}$ in. stuff is all that can be found, construct the legs and hinge area double thickness. Should two or more boards be needed to make up the required width, they can be rub jointed together.

Layout. In Figs. 2 and 3 alternative animals are shown. These are drawn on squares to enable craftsmen to reproduce the shapes easily by first drawing the graph then plotting the lines. The squares should be drawn on the wood after it has been planed and prepared. For general purposes the graph could be drawn to 2 in. squares thus making the seat height about 13 in. Naturally the over-all size could be altered to suit the age and size of the child concerned. By calling the squares $1\frac{1}{2}$ in. the seat height becomes 10 in., $2\frac{1}{2}$ in. squares produces a seat height of 16 in.

76

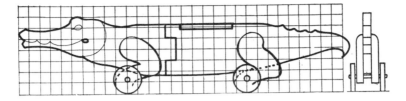

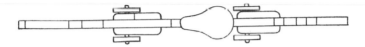

FIG. 2. CROCODILE. SIDE AND PLAN VIEWS
For the convenience of scaling, the outline is superimposed on a squared graph thereby
enabling readers to reproduce the toy to suit the child concerned

Shaping. Having obtained the timber and decided the size, the fore and aft parts, the four legs, the seat, and wheels should be carefully drawn on to the wood as already mentioned and cut out. To cut these shapes by hand would be long and tedious and we suggest that some local timber merchant having a band saw be approached to do this. Afterwards clean off the saw marks with spokeshave and rasp.

The details and the working of the hinge joining parts are shown in Fig. 4. This is done with the aid of a bolt, washers, and a piece of strap iron fitted into the part indicated and held with screws. The size of the bolt and strap is determined by the thickness of timber used. Avoid a thick bolt in thin wood.

Wheels. These are cut to size, and a $\frac{1}{2}$ in. diameter bolt used for an axle. The length of this depends upon the thickness of timber used and must be decided accordingly. Some form of spacing pieces must be fitted between the legs and wheels to keep the axle in position. Short lengths of $\frac{3}{4}$ in. electrical conduit with washers at either end will be found ideal for this if a $\frac{1}{2}$ in. bolt is used. Alternatively, $\frac{1}{2}$ in. gas or water pipe can be used, but this will be found to be rather a tight fit on the bolt. To prevent the nut working loose the outer thread could be burred over or the end drilled and a split-pin inserted. Alternatively, rubber tyred wheels complete with axle could be bought.

Seat. This should be glued and screwed into position after shaping. It could be padded and covered with a plain material, but if left bare remember to well round off the edges.

Do not forget to cut through the mouth for the guiding cord or

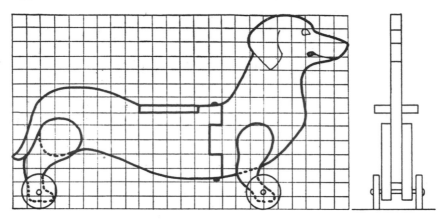

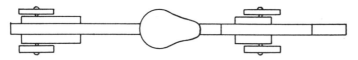

FIG. 3. ALTERNATIVE DESIGN OF A DACHSHUND
This shows that the same basic principles of construction can be applied to other animals.
Should this be contemplated, remember to well round off any pointed parts and sharp corners

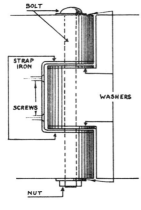

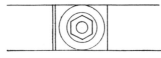

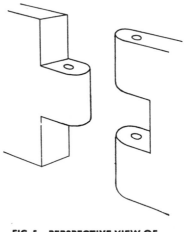

FIG. 4. ENLARGED DETAIL OF HINGE
Note use of strip iron and washers

FIG. 5. PERSPECTIVE VIEW OF HINGE

rein; this should be knotted each side of the mouth to enable the head to be turned.

Finish. A good mat oil paint should be used, or if a glossy finish is preferred, a good lacquer. The colours and the skin or fur effect and other details such as eyes, ears, etc., which will be needed to complete the effect, can be determined from coloured illustrations in children's animal books. This will require some artistic ability and should the reader not be capable of painting scales on crocodiles and fur on dogs, then an over-all colour can be given; dark green for the "croc" and middle brown for the dog. The lines of the mouth, eyes, ears, should be painted in where indicated, or better still gouged in the actual wood.

CUTTING LIST

	Long ft. in.		Wide in.	Thick in.
Crocodile—2 in. squares				
1 Piece for head part ..	2	6	12	1¾
1 Piece for tail ..	2	11	10	1¾
2 Pieces for front legs ..		10	10	1¾
2 Pieces for back legs ..	1	0	10	1¾
1 Piece for seat ..		11	7	7/8
4 Pieces for wheels ..		6	6	7/8
Dachshund—2 in. squares				
1 Piece for head	1	9	24	1¾
1 Piece for tail	2	7	14	1¾
2 Pieces for front legs ..	1	0	6	1¾
2 Pieces for back legs ..	1	1	8	1¾
1 Piece for seat ..		10	7	7/8
4 Pieces for wheels ..		6	6	7/8

Allowance has been made in lengths and widths. Thicknesses are net.

KIDDIES' SHIP ON WHEELS

THIS IS THE ideal toy where there is more than one child, because the youngsters will get any amount of fun pushing each other about. The sizes can be adapted if desired.

Top and bottom. These can be cut out of any wood of suitable thickness—$\frac{1}{2}$ in. to $\frac{7}{8}$ in. Probably two or even three pieces will have to be jointed together in their width to enable the shape to be cut out. It is advisable to screw battens beneath to strengthen the joints. To mark out the shape draw in a centre line with straight-edge and mark in the line of the stern square with it. Pencil in the length and the greatest width (which occurs about 14 in. from the stern), and drive in nails at the bow, and stern width. Bend a thin lath of wood so that it reaches to the greatest width, and hold it in position with a nail driven in to one side. Mark round the lath with pencil and repeat for the opposite side.

Cut round with bowsaw or keyhole saw and smooth with the

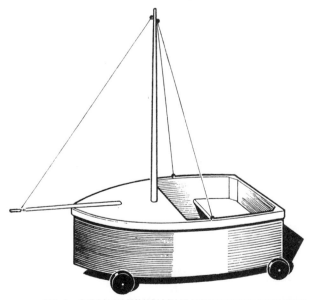

FIG. I. A TOY IN WHICH THE YOUNGSTER CAN RIDE
The ship without the bowsprit measures 3 ft. by 14 in., and is quite big enough for the small youngster. The sides are of plywood bent around a shaped top and bottom.

80

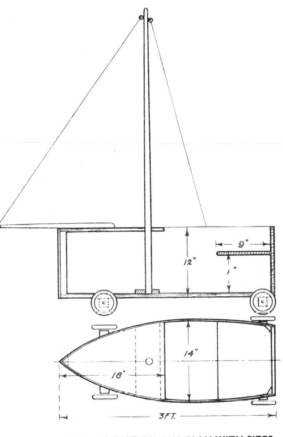

FIG. 2. ELEVATION AND PLAN WITH SIZES

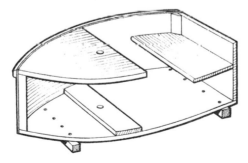

FIG. 3. HOW BOAT IS MADE

plane. Trace round the shape to mark out the top. Note from Fig. 3 that a cross-batten is fixed immediately beneath the mast.

Back and sides. A thickness similar to that of the bottom can be used for the back or stern. Fix with nails or screws and prepare the seat to the same curvature as the bottom, rounding over the front edge. An upright to be fixed at the bow must be planed to a triangular section—the angle is obtained easily by placing the wood in position on the bottom.

Cut out the sides in $\frac{1}{8}$ in. or $\frac{3}{16}$ in. plywood, the grain running vertically to simplify bending. It is advisable to allow a slight overlap for trimming. Begin the erection by fixing the bow upright between top and bottom, and nailing on a couple of temporary struts at the centre to steady the parts whilst the sides are fixed. Start at the front, fixing the ply with countersunk screws and glue. Bend the ply gradually around the sides, gluing and nailing as you proceed. When the back is reached trim off the overhang at both bow and stern and deal with the other side. A $\frac{1}{4}$ in. lath about $1\frac{1}{4}$ in. wide is fixed around the top edges all round.

Triangular blocks glued in the back corners strengthen the back joints (Fig. 3). The seat is nailed in all round. To give a suitable bearing for the wheels, squares of about $1\frac{1}{2}$ in. are screwed beneath the bottom. Long round-head screws serve to pivot the wheels. Washers are advisable on both sides. The wheels could be either of stamped metal with rubber tyres, or they could be cut out of $\frac{3}{4}$ in. or $\frac{7}{8}$ in. wood. The diameter is about $4\frac{1}{2}$ in.

The addition of the mast and bowsprit completes the boat. Ropes attached to screw eyes could be added—also sails, at any rate at the front. Back sails and ropes are best omitted as they get in the way of the child.

A rudder could be added if desired, this having a tiller screwed on at the top. Two screw eyes in the stern and two in the rudder could serve to pivot it, a dowel rod or long bolt being passed through them. Alternatively, ropes could be fitted instead of the tiller.

HOME PINBALL

ONE CAN BE fairly certain that this game will keep youngsters amused for quite a time. The pin table in Fig. 1 has the added attraction that the balls can be fed one after another to the table for play and, unless the feed wheel is removed, they cannot be taken from the table, consequently there is no chance of the balls being lost. To a worker having average skill and able to do some wood-turning, the making of the table should not be difficult, but considerable care should be taken to see that the holes in the side of the case align with the pockets in the feed wheel, otherwise the wheel will not function properly. It is also important that the surfaces on which the balls roll should be as smooth as possible.

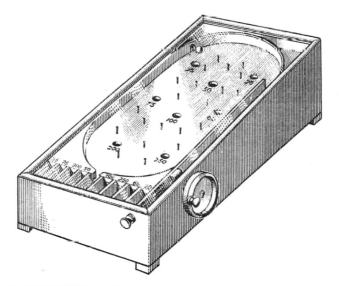

FIG. I. A GAME THAT WILL GIVE PLEASURE TO FOLK OF ALL AGES AT CHRISTMAS

The sides of the case can be put together with lap joints, but before assembly the top edges require rebating for the glass. As 21 oz. glass is $\frac{1}{10}$ in. thick, the rebates can be $\frac{1}{8}$ in. deep and $\frac{3}{16}$ in. wide. This will leave an adequate margin to receive the veneer pins which secure the capping holding the glass in place.

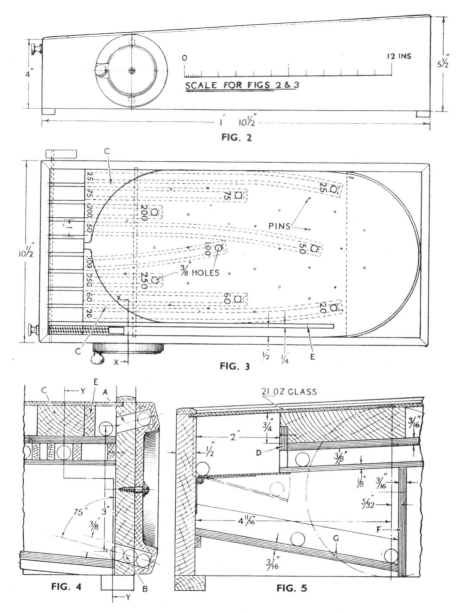

FIG. 2

FIG. 3

FIG. 4

FIG. 5

FIG. 2. SIDE ELEVATION. FIG. 3. PLAN. FIG. 4. SECTION ON X-X. FIG. 5. SECTION ON Y-Y

Holes for balls. It is advisable to bore the holes (A) and (B), Fig. 4, before assembly. After locating the centres carefully and also the centre for the screw on which the feed wheel revolves, a drilling jig can be made. This may comprise a strip of wood say 1 in. by $\frac{5}{8}$ in. through the thickness of which a $\frac{3}{8}$ in. hole is drilled at an angle of 75 degrees approximately to the surface. The screw centre is also marked on the strip and a panel pin driven through and into the screw centre marked on the side of the case.

Using the jig, one of the holes in the side is then bored, after which operation the jig can be turned through 180 degrees for boring the other hole. During the boring operations, the jig can be pinned to the side at positions where the nail holes will be hidden by the wheel. As the holes for the balls must be clean, it is suggested that a Forstner bit be used.

Feed wheel. As it is of the utmost importance that the pockets in the feed wheel shall align with the holes (A) and (B) it is suggested that the drilled side of the case should be used as a jig for boring the blind holes in the piece of stuff intended for the feed wheel. This should be a close-grained wood such as beech. The piece can be fixed to the side of the case during drilling by a screw turned into the centre marked on the side of the case. The screw should be slightly smaller in diameter than that which will be finally used. The table has been designed for $\frac{5}{16}$ in. diameter ball bearings and when drilling for the pockets care should be taken that the depth of each is such that a ball is just accommodated.

If the pockets are too deep, a ball behind the one in the lower pocket will partly project into the pocket and obstruct the turning of the wheel. Other, but smaller, holes will require to be drilled in the case, but the drilling can be done after assembly. It will be seen from Fig. 5 that the partitions of the compartments into which the balls pass after play are housed into the lower end of the case. Some trouble can be saved if these housings are cut before the case is put together.

Table. Birch plywood should be used since this material permits a smooth finish. The eight holes can be located in Fig. 3, but the positions are arbitrary, the only consideration being that the runways under the table do not have to be unduly curved. The pins are driven in after the board has been enamelled. The two lower ball guides (C) are cut so that the grain runs obliquely, in order to avoid short fibres at the tapered ends. These guides will require rebating to receive the slotted piece (D) shown in Fig. 7.

It is advisable to form the walls of the runways from $\frac{3}{16}$ in. ply, since this will allow pins being driven through the thickness of the

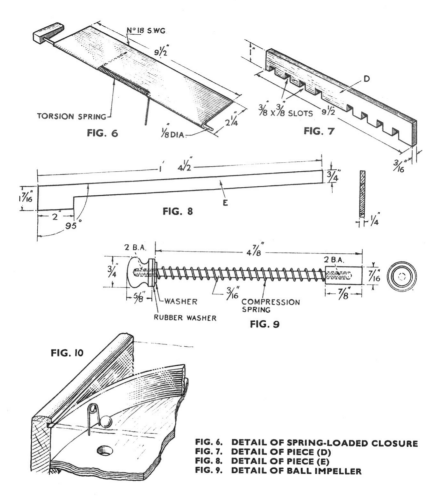

N° 18 SWG

9½"

TORSION SPRING

2¼"

FIG. 6

⅛ DIA

3/8 X 3/8 SLOTS

9½"

3/16"

D

FIG. 7

1'

4½"

3/4"

1 7/16"

2"

95°

E

FIG. 8

¼"

2 B.A.

4⅞"

2 B.A.

3/4"

5/8"

WASHER

3/16"

COMPRESSION SPRING

7/16"

7/8"

RUBBER WASHER

FIG. 9

FIG. 10

FIG. 6.   DETAIL OF SPRING-LOADED CLOSURE
FIG. 7.   DETAIL OF PIECE (D)
FIG. 8.   DETAIL OF PIECE (E)
FIG. 9.   DETAIL OF BALL IMPELLER

walls to hold them in position after gluing.   This cannot be done satisfactorily if hardboard is used.   The partitions of the ball receiving compartments can now be prepared.   It will be noted that one partition of the compartment, designated "20", is formed by a projection on the piece (E), Fig. 8.   The partitions are fixed by the housings and by veneer pins driven through the piece (D).

Having prepared the guides (C), they are glued to the table and secured by a few veneer pins from underneath.   It will be seen from Fig. 5 that the lower edge of the table is flush with the bottom of the rebates in the guides (C). In fixing the piece (E) it is advisable to prepare a small block $\frac{3}{8}$ in. wide and to use this block as a gauge when fixing the piece. This will ensure that the passageway along which the balls are propelled is uniform in width.

When these parts have been fixed, the table is inverted and packed up so that a solid support is provided. The positions of the runways are then marked and the walls glued and pinned in position. The gauge, previously used, can again be employed to obtain uniformity in the width of the channels. Where the runways are curved, it will be found advantageous to drive in a few pins into the board to retain the curve of the walls while the glue is setting. When the runways are completed, the slotted piece (D), with the partitions pinned to it, can be glued and pinned into the rebate provided for its reception. The floors of the runways are formed from a piece of $\frac{1}{8}$ in. plywood of adequate width to cover all of the runways. It will be seen from Fig. 5 that the floor projects over the lower edge of the piece (D), so that no obstruction is caused to the passage of the balls. The slots should align with the runways, and it may be found necessary to slightly trim the openings in order to secure proper alignment.

The parts now assembled constitute a unit, which is inserted in the case and the table rested on fillets glued and pinned to the sides of the case. It will be noticed that one of the walls of the runway from hole "25" is against the adjacent side of the case, which prevents the fixing of a fillet, but adequate support for the table will be provided by the fillets at the top and other long side of the case. The semi-circular wall at the top of the table will have to be fixed after the table is in place.

Spring loaded closure for ball compartments. This is cut from aluminium sheet of the gauge specified in Fig. 6. A satisfactory alternative to the use of snips for cutting is to make deep scores where the metal is to be cut and then insert the waste part of the metal in a saw kerf up to the score. If now the metal is bent first one way and then the other by applying pressure through a piece of wood held against the metal, it will soon fracture along the scores. The bead retaining the $\frac{1}{8}$ in. rod of pivoting the closure can be formed by clamping the closure between two pieces of iron in a metal vice with the edge to be bent over projecting. The rod is then laid against the projecting edge and the latter hammered over, the blows being applied to a piece of iron placed against the edge.

To finish the bead, the work is removed from the vice and laid on a flat metal surface when the partly turned-over edge can be further hammered to embrace the rod. Obviously, the space for the spring is filed out before forming the bead. The rod will have to be withdrawn to allow the insertion of the spring and, when replaced, it should be a tight fit in the bead so that it moves with the closure. The operating lever can comprise a piece of brass which is drilled to receive the end of the rod, the end being sweated in the hole.

Shoot. This is formed by a partition (F) extending across the width of the case. Abutting against the partition is an inclined floor (G) which, with the partition, forms a valley which slopes downwardly towards the hole (B), Fig. 4. It will be understood that the slope of the floor should be such that the valley has the greatest possible inclination in the space available. The floor rests on fillets as indicated in Fig. 5.

Ball impeller. The $\frac{3}{16}$ in. rod may comprise a 6 in. wire nail filed clean in the lathe and cut to length. The ends are threaded 2 B.A. to receive the knob and head, which are drilled and tapped accordingly. Boxwood is very suitable for these parts since this wood can be tapped satisfactorily.

When the impeller is in position on the board, the metal washer abuts against the inside of the case, the rubber washer being outside. This latter washer cushions the knob against the case when the impeller is released.

It is not intended that the scores allocated to the holes should necessarily be followed. It is suggested that before the glass is fixed a number of games should be played and the aggregate score noted for each hole. From the results obtained the values of the holes can be suitably accessed. Before nailing the pins into the board, it may be worth while pressing in some ordinary dress pins so that the best positions for the proper pins can be found.

It will be seen from Fig. 1 that where the upper curved wall flows into the side wall to the left of the table, that a string abutment is provided. A ball on striking the spring bounces back and rolls down the board. The path to be taken by a ball can be more or less determined by carefully adjusting the speed of the ball and consequently the amount of rebound. A safety pin which has had the guard removed will serve for this spring.

Finish. As the pin table is largely intended for use by young people, it is suggested that the table be enamelled a bright green. One of the proprietary brands of chinese lacquer will be found satisfactory.

Playing a game. Assuming that the balls have been discharged into the shoot, a player operates the feed wheel to raise a ball to the position for play on the table. When the ball has been played, the operation is repeated until the eight balls have been used. The total score obtained can then be found by adding together the values allotted to those compartments in which the balls are found. Those that have failed to score will occupy the central compartment. After the score has been recorded, the lever operating the closure of the compartment is depressed, so that the balls are again returned to the shoot ready for the next player.

SMALL BIRD HOUSE

USING $\frac{1}{2}$-IN. WOOD, the gable ends (A) will be cut from pieces 8 in. by 7 in., height to eaves being 6 in. The bird opening in front may be $2\frac{1}{2}$ in. or 3 in. in diameter. The sides (B), 8 in. by $6\frac{1}{4}$ in., butt *within* the ends, whilst a floor (C), 8 in. by 6 in., fits within the four sides of the box. The parts are nailed together and screwed through the platform (D). Note that the roof overhangs $\frac{1}{2}$ in. at the

back and about 3 in. in front. The roof parts may be cut from $\frac{1}{4}$ in. boards, $12\frac{1}{2}$ in. by $5\frac{1}{2}$ in. or 6 in. If a chimney is added, the stack may be cut from a piece $3\frac{1}{2}$ in. by 2 in. by $\frac{7}{8}$ in., with a $\frac{1}{2}$ in. length of $\frac{3}{4}$ in. dowel rod for can. The stack should pass through the roof and be halved and screwed to the house side (B). The perch, or rail,

FIG. I.   ATTRACTIVE BIRD HOUSE FOR FIXING TO THE WALL

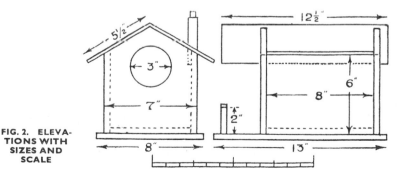

FIG. 2. ELEVATIONS WITH SIZES AND SCALE

consists of a couple (or three) $\frac{1}{2}$ in. posts 2 in. high, with a $\frac{3}{8}$ in. rail nailed across.

Door and windows may be indicated by painting. It has been stated that birds dislike red, but this we have not checked. If the box structure is fitted over the floor loose, and merely held with screws, it is easy at any time to get access to the interior for cleaning purposes.

MINIATURE TRAIN

COMPARE THIS WITH some of the crude toys offered at high prices. It has not only a realistic appearance, but is really strong. Purely as a matter of interest, the engine took two evenings only to make, the woodwork being completed in the first and the finishing in the second.

There are many additions you could make to this train: carriages, locomotive with tender, station, signal box, and so on. The simplest way is to draw them in full size so that the correct proportions are maintained.

Engine. The construction is obvious from Fig. 2. Cut out the various parts to the sizes given, trim where necessary with the plane, and rub down any roughness with glasspaper. This latter should on no account be neglected because the toy relies very largely upon the finish for its effect. Rub off any sharp angles and corners. The rounded top to the cab can be chiselled and finished with glasspaper. Use dowels for boiler, wheels, funnel, and dome. To ensure the wheels being all alike in thickness you can fix a stop to a mitre block having a square cut.

To assemble, nail the cab to the boiler, keeping it centred and the right height up from the bottom. Note that glue should be used throughout as well as nails. The strength is thereby increased enormously. Tube glue answers the purpose quite well. The base, which is $\frac{3}{16}$ in. thick, is now nailed to the cab and the saddle prepared to fit beneath the boiler. Its top surface can be hollowed with gouge or file. It is fixed at the same time as the frame block to which the

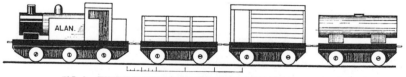

FIG. I. TINY ENGINE AND TRUCKS THAT CAN BE CUT FROM STANDARD MATERIAL

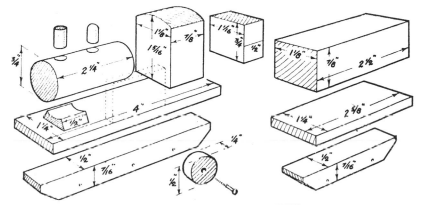

FIG. 2. THE PARTS AND THEIR SIZES

wheels are screwed. Having glued the parts, fix the base with a couple of nails to cab. Drill a hole right through frame block, base, and saddle, and knock a panel-pin right through into the boiler. In this way you avoid splitting the saddle piece.

Bore $\frac{1}{4}$ in. holes along the top of the boiler and glue in pieces of dowel to form funnel and dome. The coal bunker is fixed at the rear, and pieces of $\frac{3}{16}$ in. stuff cut to form the side tanks. Glue both bottom edges and sides of the last-named, and nail through into the boiler.

Having cut off the wheels, drill a hole in the centre of each large enough to enable them to revolve freely on the round-head screws to be used. Use $\frac{3}{4}$ in. fine gauge screws and stagger the opposite wheels slightly so that the screws do not foul each other in the thickness of the wood. It will be found that if $\frac{3}{4}$ in. screws are used they will pass nearly through the frame block.

Finishing. The simplest finish is with poster colours. These are ready for use as they are, but can be mixed with water if necessary. They are obtainable in vivid colours and cover well. They dry quite quickly. Follow with a coat of clear varnish. If spirit varnish is used it will dry rapidly. The same thing applies to shellac varnish. Oil varnish takes much longer to dry but is probably more durable. Details such as the windows, cab door, etc., can be painted in black. Complete all painting before varnishing.

Trucks. From the instructions given for the engine the trucks can be made easily. A solid block can be used for the truck portion itself, this being mounted upon a base and frame block similar to that of the engine. For the oil tank a piece of dowel can be used. The guard's van is a solid block and a separate end piece, with a piece of veneer or even card bent around the top and glued down.

THE ROCKING HORSE stands pre-eminent amongst children's toys, but that shown complete at Fig. 1 and described here marks a vast improvement in design, construction, strength, and convenience over the older types. Notwithstanding this superiority, the construction will not be found elaborate or prolonged, and the toy (built up in the way described) will appeal to the imagination of the modern child because it closely follows the form and action of the animal it represents.

Body. The advantages derived from building up the toy are not confined to strength and appearance, but, as smaller pieces of wood will be required, also enable it to be economically produced. It will be necessary to enlarge the pattern shown at Fig. 2 to full size, this being easily accomplished by ruling a number of 1 in. squares on a piece of stiff paper or thin plywood to correspond with those in the copy, and then filling in the lines of the design. From this it will be a simple matter to obtain separate patterns for the various parts.

FIG. I. BUILT-UP ROCKING HORSE
Length over Rockers, 2 ft. 6 in.

Deal of 1 in. thickness is a suitable wood, each built-up side requiring a body piece (A), head (B), foreleg (C) and hind leg (D). The legs are lapped, glued and screwed to the body piece, and the head is screwed on the inside according to the particulars shown at Fig. 3.

The rockers are next made. They should be 2 ft. 6 in. long by 4 in. deep, the curved edge being set out with a radius of 3 ft. 3 in., as suggested in Fig. 2.

At this stage the width will have to be determined, and 10 in. (measuring over the rockers) will be found suitable, although 12 in. could be allowed if desired. A foot-rest measuring 1 ft. 4 in. long by 3 in. wide should be fitted over and fixed to the rockers at the width desired.

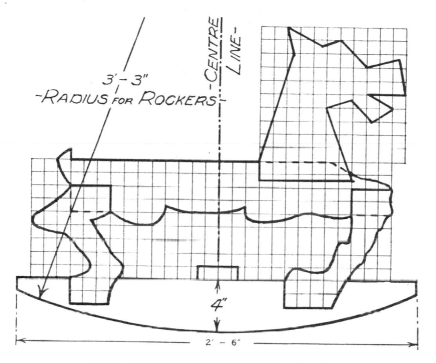

3' — 3"
-RADIUS for ROCKERS-

-CENTRE LINE-

4"

2' — 6"

FIG. 2. THE HORSE PLOTTED OUT INTO I in. SQUARES

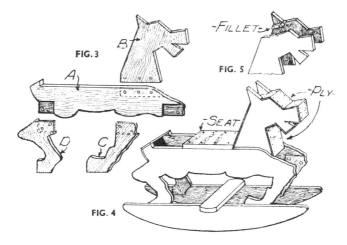

FIG. 3

B

-FILLET-

FIG. 5

A

-PLY-

-SEAT

D

C

FIG. 4

FIG. 3. HORSE PARTS. FIG. 4. ASSEMBLING. FIG. 5. HEAD

Seat. The seat is fixed over the body pieces. It should fit tight against the small projections at the back, but at the front a space of $\frac{3}{16}$ in. must be allowed.

The process of covering the body with plywood may then be proceeded with as shown in Fig. 4. Pieces of ply are nailed around the hind quarters, and around the head, the mouth being left open. The piece which runs back between the ears will require to be supported by nailing small fillets inside the head, as shown in the sketch at Fig. 4. All the joints could be glued as well as nailed, and in finally finishing the edges could be neatly rounded.

It is a good plan to cover the seat to make it more comfortable. It could be stuffed with hair or any old waste material could be used, a covering of leather cloth or suitable material being drawn taut over it and tacked. Reins and harness can be made from leather straps or from gimp. A girth too can be cut out and tacked on. All painting should be completed first. Round over all edges beforehand. This will necessitate the nails being well punched in. Fill in the holes with plastic wood.

BACKYARD SANDBOX

MANY CRUDE ARRANGEMENTS for providing a "sand playground" for the youngster are to be seen, and the roughest contrivance will serve the purpose if no objection is taken to a structure that may be unsightly. We show a form of combined box and table which may be folded up overnight, and removed to an outhouse for storage in winter. Later, when the child is beyond the sand age, the box will come in useful for seedlings, etc.

Only a suggestion is necessary. The form shown need not be followed in detail, the size depending on one's own requirements, and the construction largely on the material available. This, if

FIG. I. SANDBOX FOR
THE CHILDREN
The double top folds back to
form tables or seats

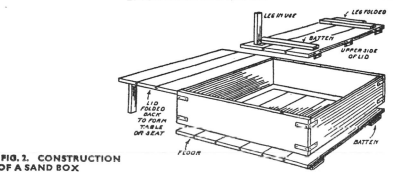

LEG IN USE

LEG FOLDED

BATTEN

UPPER SIDE OF LID

LID FOLDED BACK TO FORM TABLE OR SEAT

FLOOR

BATTEN

FIG. 2. CONSTRUCTION OF A SAND BOX

bought rough, may be planed just sufficiently to prevent a child's limbs from encountering splinters.

The box indicated was made about 3 ft. 6 in. square, being built of four sides, 3 ft. 6 in. by 9 in., nailed together and additionally held by heavy steel trunk corners. The floor was of tongued and grooved boarding, nailed on. Below, two $4\frac{1}{2}$ in. by $\frac{7}{8}$ in. battens were screwed across as shown. These are desirable not only for strength, but also for raising the floor off the grass.

The hinged tops, apart from acting as lids, serve either as tables or seats when folded back. This of course adds greatly to the usefulness of the box which, without being filled with sand, provides (in the size indicated) a play-pen which will accommodate as many as four youngsters. The tops, or lids (Fig. 2) will be approximately 3 ft. 6 in. by 1 ft. 9 in., each made up of tongued and grooved matchboard with $2\frac{1}{2}$ in. by $\frac{7}{8}$ in. battens screwed on. (Note that these battens are screwed on the *upper* face when the lid is *closed*.) Each lid is hinged with three stout butts which, of course, will necessarily show on the outside.

To provide legs for the lids when opened back, four short lengths of 2 in. by $\frac{7}{8}$ in. stuff will serve. The length will depend on the width of box sides. The legs may conveniently be fitted to lie alongside (and outside) the lid battens, and should be hinged with stout back-flap hinges.

When the lids are open and in use either as tables or seats there is little chance of the legs bending inwards. Any risk of this may be obviated by very slightly bevelling the hinged end of each leg so that it shows a gentle outward splay when on the ground. Turnbuttons may be screwed to the battens to keep the legs in position when down.

As already stated, the box may be any size; 2 ft. 6 in. square is about the minimum and 3 ft. 6 in. is a useful average. Alternatively, it might be oblong, say, 4 ft. by 2 ft. 9 in.

DOLL CARRIAGE

THE CONSTRUCTION OF the body is given in Fig. 5.

Body. There are two side frames put together with halved joints, joined by four-cross-rails. To enable the rail sizes and shape of sides to be obtained the side view of the body should be drawn in full size on a piece of paper. Sketch in the elliptical shape and mark in the positions of the rails. Top and bottom rails are obvious, and the sloping ones can be set at whatever angle best suits the shape. The chief point is to have enough overlap to give good halving joints.

Cut out the wood, and, placing the parts on the drawing, mark in the shoulders by drawing a pencil along where they cross each other. A lot of the waste can be cut away before marking in and cutting the halved joints. It saves unnecessary sawing. Mark in the depth with the gauge, using the latter from the face side in every case. Glue the joints and put thumbscrews on them. When set mark out and cut the shape, cleaning up with spokeshave. Cut out the cross-rails and glue and nail them in position. Note that those at the bottom should stand proud of the shape so that they can be levelled afterwards.

Covering. The thinnest possible material should be used. Plywood 1·5 mm. thick is ideal and can often be obtained. It should be used with the grain running crosswise. Plastic board can be

FIG. 1.

96

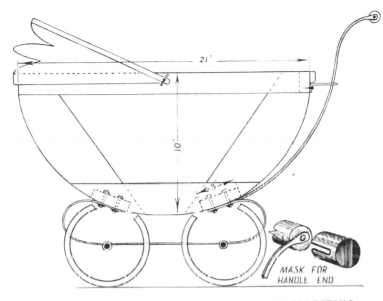

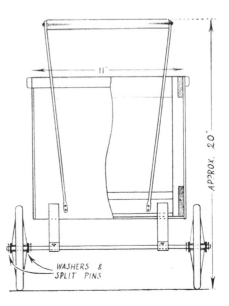

MASK FOR
HANDLE END

FIG. 2 SIDE ELEVATION WITH MAIN SIZES, AND HANDLE DETAILS

WASHERS &
SPLIT PINS

FIG. 3. END ELEVATION

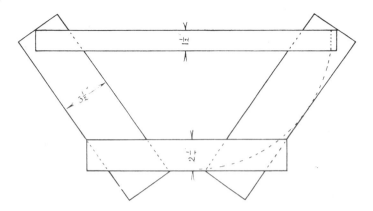

FIG. 4. HOW BODY SIDE FRAMES ARE MADE

FIG. 5. BODY PARTS ASSEMBLED

**FIG. 6. HOW SPRINGS
ARE FIXED**

bought $\frac{1}{16}$ in. thick and is also suitable. Failing this use thin aluminium sheet. The latter will have to be screwed on. The other materials are glued, and if plastic board is chosen it should be well roughened first to give a key. Allow it to stand out about $\frac{1}{16}$ in. so that it can be levelled afterwards.

Complete the curved portion first, and, if possible, have it in a single piece. If joints are unavoidable arrange them in line with the bottom cross-rails. When the glue has set level the edges and add the side panels. Seats can be added as required. They are arranged to rest upon battens, but are not fixed finally until after lining.

Chassis. Use $\frac{3}{4}$ in. by $\frac{1}{16}$ in. strip iron for springs. To ensure both being the same shape they should be bent around a piece of wood sawn to the inside shape. They are bolted to the bottom cross-rails as in Fig. 2. Axles are fixed to them by means of metal clips riveted or bolted on as in Fig. 6. Axles are of mild steel rod of a diameter to suit the wheels, generally $\frac{3}{8}$ in. The wheels are held in position by cotter pins passed through holes drilled right through the axles with large washers at each side to give easy movement. Alternatively square axles with rounded ends can be obtained.

Handles are of $\frac{1}{4}$ in. or $\frac{5}{16}$ in. mild steel rod bent to shape around a rounded object and hammered. Both ends are beaten flat for fixing, that at top at right angles with the other as it has to fit the handle. It is easily beaten flat if first made red hot. First, however, the brackets for fixing at the top should be made and slipped on. A 1 in. dowel rod is used for the handle, and the ends are cut in to enable the metal rods to be flush. Either screws with decorative heads should be used for fixing, or cover caps made as in Fig. 2.

Painting and lining. Give a coat of priming, follow with an undercoat, and finally a gloss coat. The lining is fixed to battens screwed around the top of the body. Tack the material to the underside of the battens, and pass it over the top to the inside. A layer of cotton wool, linters' felt, or plain rag stuffing gives a springy inside finish. Gimp fixed with covered nails makes a neat finish.

Hood. The main front hoop is of flat strip iron with holes drilled

CUTTING LIST

			Long ft.	in.	Wide in.	Thick in.
2 Side rails	..	..	1	$9\frac{1}{2}$	$1\frac{3}{4}$	$\frac{3}{4}$
2 Side rails	..	..	1	$2\frac{1}{2}$	$2\frac{1}{2}$	$\frac{3}{4}$
4 Side rails	..	..	1	$2\frac{1}{2}$	$3\frac{3}{4}$	$\frac{3}{4}$
2 Cross-rails	..	..		10	$1\frac{3}{4}$	$\frac{3}{4}$
2 Cross-rails	..	..		10	$3\frac{1}{4}$	$\frac{3}{4}$
2 Battens	..	..	1	$10\frac{1}{4}$	1	$\frac{3}{8}$
2 Battens	..	..		$11\frac{1}{2}$	1	$\frac{3}{8}$
1 Handle	..	..		9	(dowel)	1
Metal parts						
2 Springs	..	..	2	6	$\frac{3}{4}$	$\frac{1}{16}$
2 Axles	..	..	1	3	$\frac{5}{16}$ or $\frac{3}{8}$ in. dia.	
2 Handles	..	..	1	8	$\frac{1}{4}$ or $\frac{5}{16}$ in. dia.	
2 Hoops	..	..	3	0	$\frac{1}{2}$ about $\frac{1}{16}$ in.	
2 Wires	..	..	3	0	$\frac{1}{8}$ in. dia.	

Lengths and widths allow for trimming. Thicknesses are net.

at the ends to enable it to be pivoted. The other hoops (one or two) can be in stout wire looped at the ends for the same purpose. Open the hood and tie string across to keep in the open position. Cut the material to suit the shape, allowing sufficient for the seams. Sew the parts together and fix to the hoops with large stitches. The pivoting is on bolts passed through the body from inside. The bolts should have squares beneath the head to prevent turning, and they should preferably be fixed before lining. The hood stays pass over the bolts and are held by wing nuts. At the back the hood is held by a couple of screws.

KIDDIES' HAMMERING TOY

ALL CHILDREN LOVE to get busy with a hammer, but they can do quite a lot of damage. Here is a toy in which they can hammer away without any harm. The pellets are knocked into the hole at the top, and are driven out at the end. They pass through an interior channel, lining up one behind the other, the pressure from the last pellet knocked in driving out the first one.

The illustrations opposite show how the toy works and how it is made. A channel is cut in the main block and a plywood side screwed or nailed to it to enclose the channel. A metal spring is screwed into a little recess in the top of the channel to offer a slight resistance to the pellets, otherwise the latter would pass through too easily. It is raised by the pellets as they pass through.

Construction. Plane up the main block to the sizes given, and cut the channel. Much of the waste can be removed by boring a series of holes along the length. A gouge is useful to follow, and finally a chisel. It is a good idea to prepare the pellets—say half a dozen—to make sure that they pass through without jamming. A chip removed here and there will ease matters.

The spring can be cut from an old clock spring, or any other suitable metal can be used. Two holes must be drilled through it to take the fixing screw. To drill the holes heat the end of the spring to a cherry red and allow to cool naturally. This will soften the steel. Hold the latter with a damp rag to prevent the heat from travelling along and taking out the temper along the whole length.

Nail on the plywood side, and cut out the two ends and the top piece. The latter fits in grooves cut across the ends. Before fixing cut a hole in one end to line up with the end of the channel. When

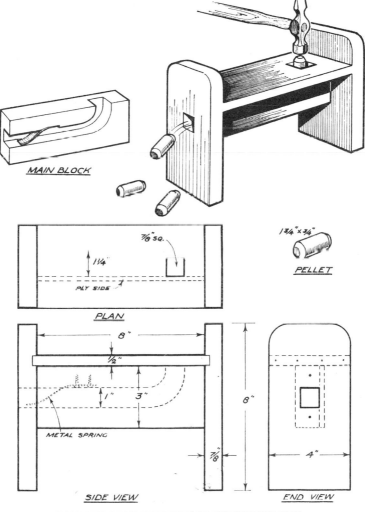

MAIN BLOCK

7/8" SQ.

1¼"

PLY SIDE

PLAN

1¾" × ¾"

PELLET

8"

½"

1"

3"

8"

METAL SPRING

7/8"

SIDE VIEW

4"

END VIEW

SIZES AND CONSTRUCTION OF HAMMERING TOY

complete put the whole thing together with glue and nails. Punch in the nails and fill in the holes with plastic wood. Level down the joints and take off all sharp angles and corners with glasspaper. Finish with oil paint.

For the pellets short lengths of ¾ in. dowel rod can be used. It is necessary to chamfer the ends as shown opposite so that the pellets pass around the curve easily.

WHEELBARROW

THIS IS AN ever-popular toy amongst children. If you can get a ready-made wheel, wood or iron, by all means use it. Otherwise it is quite simple to make one from solid wood, laminating two pieces with the grain at right angles for strength.

As a toy is invariably painted, practically any kind of wood can be used, providing that it is reasonably free from knots. Using 1 in. square stuff, make a frame as shown in Fig. 2. Draw the shape in full size so that the adjustable bevel can be set to the required angle. This will enable the ends of the cross-rails to be marked; also the shallow notches in which they fit. The ends forming the handles can either be left straight and rounded over, or pieces can be glued on beneath as in Fig. 4 to enable the shape to be worked.

Put the parts together with glue and nails and bore holes at the front to take the axle. Judge it as closely as possible and bore right

FIG. I. PRESENT SUITABLE FOR EITHER BOY OR GIRL

This is always a popular toy with the youngsters, and, if attractively finished in bright colours, has a strong appeal. Sizes are 24 in. long over the frame by about 12 in. wide

through the one piece. Repeat on the other rail and then allow the bit to pass right across to correct any inaccuracy. Fig. 5 shows how the wheel is made from two $\frac{1}{2}$ in. thicknesses, the grain at right angles. Bore a hole half-way in from each side to take a tightly-fitting iron axle rod, and add a $\frac{1}{2}$ in. circular block at each side as in Fig. 5 to stiffen it. Fig. 5 also shows how the ends of the frame rails are cut away to enable the axle to be fitted afterwards.

For the body use wood about $\frac{1}{4}$ in. thick. Prepare the bottom to the sizes in Fig. 3 to fit on the framework, standing in a trifle. All edges will have to be bevelled, but this is best done after the sides have been added. The angles at which the ends of the long sides are planed are not important. Since the bottom edges are a trifle over 12 in. long, the top edges might be about 18 in. Cut to shape,

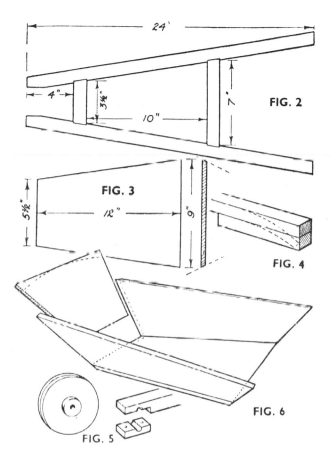

FIG. 2

FIG. 3

FIG. 4

FIG. 5

FIG. 6

MAIN SIZES AND DETAILS OF CONSTRUCTION

and bevel the bottom edges of both to give the required slope. They must be alike.

Fix to the bottom with glue and nails, and fit the front end as in Fig. 6, noting the edges must be at an angle. Cut the top to a curve, and fix again with glue and nails. Follow with the rear end. Level the edges and either nail or screw to the frame.

The legs are notched to fit over the rails, and are taken off at an angle to line up with the slope of the sides. Fix with a screw through each rail, and nail through the body at the top.

HOW TO MAKE A XYLOPHONE

THIS HAS BECOME an extremely popular instrument in recent years, and the work of making it is most interesting. The example in Fig. 1 consists of twenty-seven notes, ranging from G to A. If carefully made of suitable wood a perfectly practical instrument is possible with good tone. There is nothing difficult about the work, though a good ear is needed for tuning. We are greatly indebted to Messrs. Boosey & Hawkes Ltd., manufacturers of musical instruments, for much of the information in this article.

FIG. I. COMPLETED INSTRUMENT FOR PLAYING ON A TABLE OR FOR FIXING TO A STAND
It has a range of over two octaves. Middle C is the fourth note from the left in the front row

Easily the best wood for the keys is Honduras rosewood. This has a ring about it that no other wood seems to possess. It may, however, be difficult to obtain, and it is then a case of falling back upon a timber of comparable weight and quality. The instrument in Fig. 1 has notes of purpleheart, which gives quite good results but has not the quality of rosewood. Readers may like to experiment with other timbers which they can get. Honduras rosewood has a weight of about 60 lb. per cubic foot, and anything much lighter than this is not likely to be so successful. The following are the weights of timber of a similar class: satinwood 59–64 lb., cocus 74 lb., boxwood 54–70 lb. Any of these would be worth experimenting with, though we can only repeat that professional makers have never found a timber to equal Honduras rosewood.

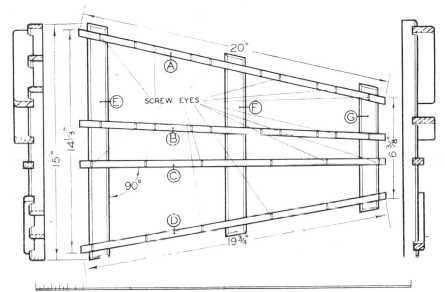

FIG. 2.   CONSTRUCTION OF FRAME

Note that only the member (C) is at right angles with the cross pieces (E), (F) and (G)

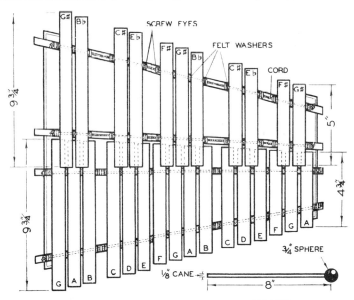

FIG. 3.   POSITION OF KEYS ON THE FRAMEWORK

They are not fixed tightly.   The cord with spacing washers holds them in place

The stand can be made of any straight-grained timber. That in Fig. 1 is of Parana pine. The converging members fit into notches cut in the three cross-pieces and are held with screws driven in from beneath. Strips of felt glued to the top edges provide a suitable bed for the keys to rest on.

Stand. Sizes of this are given in Fig. 2. It is a help to set out the whole thing on a sheet of brown paper or plywood as this gives the exact angles at which the various grooves are cut. Note that of the four members on which the keys rest (A, B, C, and D), only C requires a square groove. The grooves for all the others are at an angle, all varying.

Plane up the four pieces (A, B, C, and D), to finish $\frac{3}{8}$ in. thick.

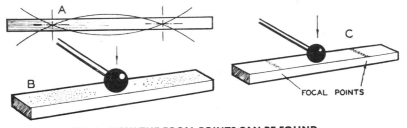

FIG. 4. HOW THE FOCAL POINTS CAN BE FOUND
There is no need to test each note in this way if the sizes in Fig. 3 are followed, but when drilling the holes some slight variation is permissible to enable the keys to be placed in alignment on the frame

Those which support the black notes (A and B) are $1\frac{1}{4}$ in. wide, the others (C and D) $\frac{5}{8}$ in. wide. In this way the black notes stand up above the others.

By placing the cross-pieces (E, F, and G), on the full-size drawing the exact positions of the grooves can be marked; also the angles. Note that each set of notches is at the same angle. Thus all those to hold piece A are at the same angle; and so on.

The grooves being cut with saw and chisel, all the grooves in the cross-pieces are drilled for the screws. The latter should be of fine gauge so that they do not split the thin wood, and for the same reason the thread holes should be bored to the full depth.

Any of the usual finishes can be used for the stand—french polish, varnish, or cellulose. It is a help to apply this when the parts are separate and to assemble later.

To hold the cords on which the notes are threaded screw eyes are driven in in the positions shown in Fig. 3. Strips of felt are glued between these, any varnish or polish being scraped away beforehand. Felt can sometimes be obtained in strips, but it may have to be cut from a wide sheet.

Keys. All of them are $\frac{3}{4}$ in. wide by $\frac{1}{2}$ in. thick. The length varies according to the note; the shorter it is the higher the note. The sizes in Fig. 3 can be followed, though it should be realised that each has to be tuned afterwards. Plane up the wood in strips and cross-cut to the lengths given. Mark on the back of each the note it is supposed to be—A, C sharp, and so on.

Each has to be drilled in two places to take the cord, and there are ideally exact positions known as the focal points for the holes. The latter should certainly approximate to these, though anything like micrometer accuracy is quite unnecessary. A variation of as much as $\frac{1}{8}$ in. or so does not affect the note much. If the positions in Fig. 3 are followed they will not be greatly out.

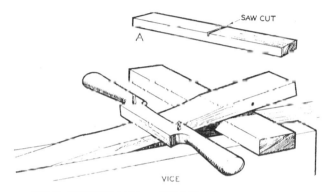

FIG. 5.   TRIMMING THE NOTE FOR CORRECT PITCH
Hollowing the underside has the effect of flattening the note.   Trimming the ends sharpens it

These focal points represent positions in the keys where there is practically no vibration. When a key is struck it vibrates as shown in great exaggeration by the curved lines (A, Fig. 4). The points where the curves cross each other are the focal points. You can test this for yourself by putting some fine dust on a key as at B, Fig. 4, and striking with the hammer. The dust will tend to concentrate in the region of the focal points as at C. The effect is more noticeable in a metal key than in a wood one.

Tuning. Having drilled the holes—noting that, except those opposite strip C, they are at an angle, which follows the slope of the pieces (A, B, C, D)—the edges and corners are rounded and finished with glasspaper.

If a test is now made all the notes will appear sharp, possibly by a tone or even two tones. To lower the note reverse it and take shavings from the middle with a spokeshave as in Fig. 5. The amount to be removed can soon be ascertained by trial and error. Tuning against a piano is the simplest method. If by any chance too much is removed so that the note is flat it can be corrected by taking shavings from the end of the note to reduce its length. This, however, should be unnecessary.

An alternative to flattening the note by shavings is to make a saw cut across the lower surface as at A, Fig. 5. When tuning is completed give the keys a coat of clear varnish or clear cellulose. Each is marked with the note it represents. Paint on the marks at the ends where they are not normally struck with the beaters.

Fitting up. Tie a knot at one end of a length of cord and thread a felt washer on to it. Pass it through the end screw eye, put on another washer, and thread on the first note. Continue the process until the next screw eye is reached. In the case of the black notes it is necessary to tie knots in the cord so that there are wide spaces between B♭ and C♯, E♭ and F♯.

Beaters. These can be spheres of boxwood or hard rubber about ⅞ in. diameter mounted on cane handles.

BLACKBOARD AND EASEL

CHILDREN WILL SCRIBBLE so it is far better to encourage a budding artist by providing something on which it can be done rather than by chastising youngsters for their efforts upon the house walls. It does not cost much and is simple to make, giving pleasure and amusement to boys and girls. The girls can turn it into a little tea-time table as shown in the sketch, Fig. 2.

The board is ⅜ in. thick plywood or laminated board with rounded corners and rounded edges. The sizes given in Fig. 4 are only offered as a guide. Any piece of board near to the sizes will do. The best finish is the special blackboard paint made for the purpose. Alternatively finish by staining board with ebony water stain. Rub down and re-stain if necessary. Leave for 24 hours. Add to one pint of drop black in turps a dessertspoonful of gold size. Stir in two tablespoonfuls of fine ground carborundum powder. Add second coat 12 hours after first.

The easel is made from 2 in. by ¾ in. deal or whitewood and, when finished, is painted and enamelled a cream or buff colour. The cross rails are tenoned to the uprights the tenons being about 1 in. long and for extra strength the tenons could be pegged with dowels driven through. The front uprights are semi-circular at the top while the rear uprights are cut square with the upper edge of the top rail.

Holes for the pegs are drilled through the front uprights a suitable distance apart and the two frames are then hinged together at the top with a pair of 2 in. brass butt-hinges. The 12 in. rule-joint stay shown in Fig. 4 keeps the easel steady when opened and there is little danger of its being knocked over on to the younger members of the

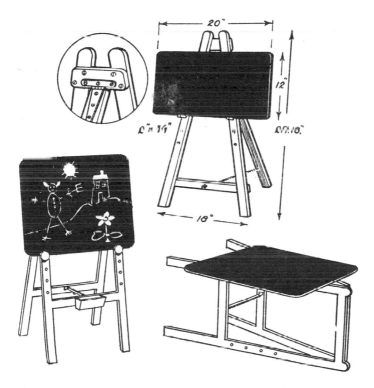

FIG. 1. BLACKBOARD IN NORMAL USE. FIG. 2. IN USE AS A TABLE
FIG. 3 (top). A SIMPLER DESIGN TO MAKE

family in a rumpus. The same thing applies to the pegs. These are shown in Fig. 4 with a large diameter disc to the front which prevents the board from tilting forward upon the heads of the tiny tots. These discs should be well wedged to the pegs.

As it is difficult to obtain rule-joint stays with two bent ears a method is shown whereby the flat ear can be screwed to a small block which is, in turn, screwed to the cross rail of the easel. If stays with two bent ears are obtainable then the block is not necessary, Fig. 5. A small chalk-box in tin or plywood will be useful and save much labour upon the floor.

CUTTING LIST

	Long ft. in.		Wide in.	Thick in.
2 Front Uprights	3	3	2	$\frac{3}{4}$
2 Back Uprights	3	2	2	$\frac{3}{4}$
4 Cross rails..	1	5	2	$\frac{3}{4}$
1 Board	2	2	22	$\frac{3}{8}$

All sizes are net.

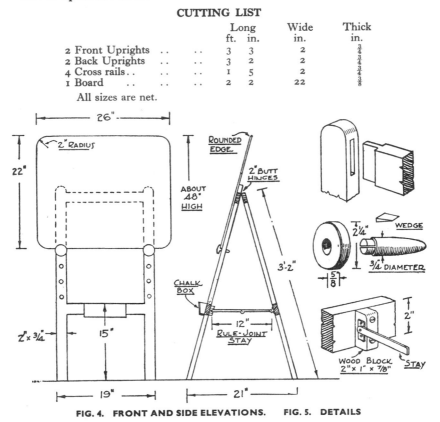

FIG. 4. FRONT AND SIDE ELEVATIONS.   FIG. 5. DETAILS

A simpler pattern which does not require any special joints to be cut is given in Fig. 3.   In this the easel is in tripod form.   Cut out the parts to length and mark where the horizontals cross the uprights. Round over the ends where necessary.   At this stage do not bother about cutting the ends of the horizontals at an angle.   Bore the screw holes and fix all parts together, two screws to each joint as in Fig. 3. The ends of the horizontals can then be cut off in line with the uprights and be levelled.   A hinge, preferably of the cross-garnet type is used to hinge the back strut.   A piece of cord threaded through holes prevents the easel from opening too far.   The legs can be plain dowels.

TABLE BOWLING

FLOOR SKITTLES HAVE the disadvantage, where children are
concerned, that damage is likely to be caused by the ball if the game
is played in a room. This cannot happen with the table game since
the ball is anchored to a cord. In the game shown here the skittles

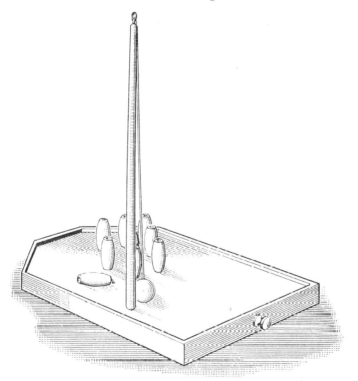

AMUSING INDOOR GAME FOR THE WINTER MONTHS
The skittles themselves have cords attached to the undersides. To stand them up after
play it is merely necessary to pull the handle at the front

are connected by cord to a yoke which can be pulled against the
action of a spring to set them up again after having been knocked
down. The feature has the added advantage that the skittles cannot
be separated from the board and be lost.

111

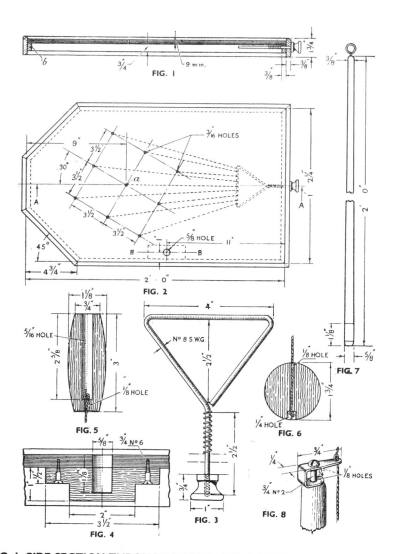

FIG. 1

FIG. 2

FIG. 5

FIG. 3

FIG. 4

FIG. 6

FIG. 7

FIG. 8

FIG. 1. SIDE SECTION THROUGH BOARD. FIG. 2. PLAN VIEW WITH MAIN SIZES. FIG. 3. WIRE YOKE. FIG. 4. BLOCK ON UNDERSIDE TO SUPPORT POST. FIG. 5. SECTION THROUGH PIN. FIG. 6. BALL SECTION. FIG. 7. POST DETAIL. FIG. 8. EFFECTIVE ATTACHMENT FOR CORD AT TOP OF POST.

The board is best made from 9 mm. birch plywood since this material will remain level, and, as it has a close grain, a nice finish can be obtained if enamelled. As the skittles receive rough treatment, they should be turned from a hardwood such as beech or birch. In all probability a wooden ball about $1\frac{3}{4}$ in. diameter can be purchased, but if one has to be turned it need not be perfectly spherical. For the post, $\frac{5}{8}$ in. dowelling will be found satisfactory.

A suggested material for the yoke is No. 8 S.W.G. galvanised iron wire, since this can be bent cold in the vice and, although its diameter is a little smaller than that of a 2 B.A. thread, an adequate thread can be worked at the end to take the knob. A suitable compression spring may be at hand, but if not, one can be purchased from a firm which specialises in the manufacture of springs. If a piece of boxwood or ebony can be found for the knob, so much the better, since the knob will have to be tapped No. 2 B.A. in the end grain to take the yoke. The grain of beech is hardly dense enough to permit threading.

Construction. Referring to Fig. 2, it will be seen that the dimensions are given over the board excluding the edging as it is believed that this will simplify setting out. If the centre hole a is first located, it will be found that it is an easy matter to set out the positions of the other holes. In order to prevent the cords chafing when they pass through the holes, these should be countersunk as indicated in Fig. 1. The particular arrangement of the holes enables the cords to be clear of each other and the spacing permits the skittles to be knocked over without fouling each other. By avoiding the alignment of three skittles with the length of the board, the game is made more difficult and interesting.

As the post must stand firmly upright, it is made a tight fit in the $\frac{5}{8}$ in. hole indicated in Fig. 2. The thickness of the board does not allow a blind hole of adequate depth to be bored for the post, and therefore a piece shown in Fig. 4 is screwed and glued under the board before boring the hole.

So that a good fixing for the $1\frac{3}{4}$ in. by $\frac{3}{8}$ in. edging may be provided, a fillet b is glued and pinned around the edges of the board. When this is fixed, the edges should be cleaned up and carefully tested for squareness. The edging is glued and pinned to the fillet, the abutting ends being mitred. It adds to the appearance of the board if the top edge of the edging is rounded as shown. An $\frac{11}{64}$ in. hole will have to be drilled to receive the shank of the yoke and this hole should be so positioned that the yoke will be just clear of the undersurface of the board, but allowing free movement of the spring.

It will be found that a 15 in. length of No. 8 S.W.G. galvanised wire will suffice for the yoke. No difficulty should be experienced in bending it to shape in the vice, but care should be taken to see that the shank part is straight and central with the triangular part. The gauge of the wire does not permit a full 2 B.A. thread to be cut on the end of the shank, but an adequate thread can be cut with a die, to enable the attachment of the knob.

Pins. A 2 ft. 8 in. length of hardwood such as beech or birch about $1\frac{3}{8}$ in. square will be required for the skittles. The length is cross cut to provide nine pieces each about $3\frac{1}{2}$ in. long. After marking the diagonals at the ends of each piece, central $\frac{1}{8}$ in. holes are bored to a depth of $\frac{1}{2}$ in. at both ends of each piece. At one end of each piece the $\frac{1}{8}$ in. hole is counterbored $\frac{5}{16}$ in. diameter as shown in Fig. 5. A mandrel is next turned to fit the $\frac{5}{16}$ in. hole in each piece so that each in turn can be turned between centres. The back centre of the lathe will, of course, be centred in the $\frac{1}{8}$ in. hole left for the cord. The lower end of each skittle should be slightly dished as indicated so that the skittle will stand firmly.

The ball can be turned in a similar manner to that employed for the skittles, but there is no need to get the ball precisely spherical.

Attaching the cords. In connecting the cords to the yoke, sufficient slackness should be allowed so that the skittles will be free to fall over after having been struck by the ball. But this slackness should not be such that the yoke has to be fully pulled back to set the skittles on their ends again. The spring acts to return the yoke to its original position, so that there is always the right amount of slackness to permit the skittles to fall.

The cord from which the ball is suspended is shown attached to a screweye fixed in the top of the post, but an alternative method of attachment is illustrated in Fig. 8. The fitment shown comprises a piece of strip metal, tinplate for instance, cut to the shape indicated and mounted on the post by a screw, which passes through clearance holes in the fitment. Thus the fitment is free to pivot about the screw and any tendency for the cord to wind around the post is prevented.

The completed article can be made attractive in appearance by enamelling the parts using one of the proprietary brands of lacquer.

THE PLAY SHOP

A SHOP BIG enough for children actually to play in is always popular. It runs into rather a lot of material, but those who have the plywood or hardboard will find it well worth while. The sides are hinged so that the whole thing will fold flat. Shelves and counter too, are detachable. Any kind of trade can be represented—in fact two or three boards, such as BAKER, BUTCHER, CHEMIST, etc., can be prepared, so giving the children a change.

FIG. I. MADE FROM PLYWOOD OR FIBRE BOARD AND APPLIED STRIPS
The suggested size of 4 ft. 6 in. long by 2 ft. 6 in. deep by 4 ft. 6 in. high is convenient in most cases, but a little larger or smaller would not make much difference

Construction. Cut out three pieces of plywood or fibre board—whatever is available—to the sizes given in Fig. 2, and mark out the position of the door and window. Actually the exact sizes do not matter a great deal, but those shown do give an idea of what are good working proportions. The door might be some 3 ft. 3 in. high by 15 in. wide, and the opening can be marked out and cut to this size. In the case of the window, however, the glass has necessarily to fit

115

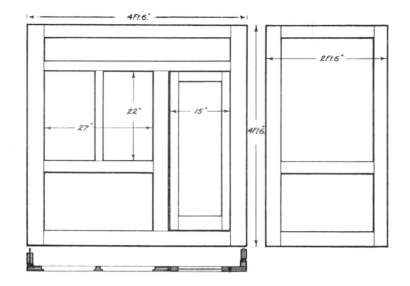

FIG. 2. FRONT ELEVATION WITH SECTIONAL PLAN, AND ELEVATION OF SIDE

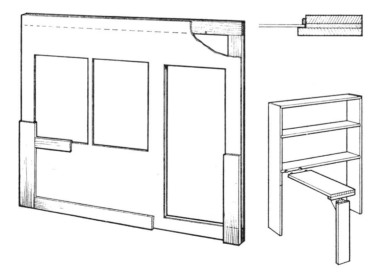

FIG 3. HOW STRIPS ARE APPLIED TO THE MAIN BOARD.   **FIG. 4. SHELVES AND COUNTER**

in a rebate, and, since this is formed by allowing the front battens to overlap the edges, the openings in the main board must be cut about $\frac{3}{8}$ in. full all round. This is shown clearly in Fig. 3.

To cut the openings it is necessary to bore holes to enable the keyhole saw to be started. When this has sawn a few inches the handsaw can be substituted. This cuts more quickly and keeps to the line better than the keyhole saw. When the openings are cut clean up the edges where necessary and prepare the strips. These might be 3 in. to 4 in. wide by $\frac{1}{2}$ in. thick. Enough for both front and back are needed, and note that where a joint is vertical at the front the corresponding one at the back is horizontal. The one thus stiffens the other.

Fix those at the front first, nailing through the board into the strips. Nail on the back ones right through the panel into the front strips. In this way no nails are visible at the front. Before fixing, however, it is advisable to apply the finish as it is much simpler when the parts are separate. Paint can be used throughout, or the main panel can be painted or distempered and the battens stained.

Hingeing. Provision has to be made for hingeing the sides to the front, and, to enable the whole to be flat, a batten as thick as the total thickness of the sides is screwed on at one side. This is shown in the plan section in Fig. 2. Thus when the left-hand side has been folded in, the other can close over it. The method of allowing the front battens to overlap and so form a rebate in which the glass can fit has already been mentioned. Figs. 3 and 4 show this detail clearly. The glass is held by beads fixed at the back with nails (see section above, Fig. 4).

The door can be made similarly to the main front and sides. Battens are nailed to each side of a sheet of ply or fibre board. After levelling the edges and fitting it is hinged to the right with three 2 in. hinges. If possible avoid driving the screws into the joints. The addition of the trade board completes the exterior. It can be fitted with two screw eyes at the top to engage hooks driven into the battens. Thus a fresh trade sign can always be substituted.

Interior fittings. These are shown in Fig. 4 and consist of a shelf fitment, the size of which is arranged to agree with the window, and a counter. Put the shelves together with simple grooved joints. Grooves are cut across the uprights and the shelves glued and nailed in them. At the top simple rebates are cut to hold the top shelf. The whole fitment merely stands behind the window, though hooks and eyes could be added for security.

The counter is held in position with hooks which engage in screw eyes entered into the bottom shelf. At the free end a cross-batten is fixed underneath and an upright strut hinged to it. To prevent it from closing by an accidental knock with the foot a triangular strut is hinged to the underside of the counter. Thus the whole thing can be folded flat when not in use.

Goods to sell in the shop can consist of ordinary small cartons and packets in which goods are normally sold, but many additional ones can be made in wood, such as loaves, joints, cakes, etc. When painted they look very realistic. A tin of sand can be kept to represent sugar to be weighed out. A pair of scales is given on page 37.

If preferred this toy could be made in the form of a dwelling-house rather than a shop. The general construction and sizes could be similar to those shown here. The windows, of course, would be considerably smaller than for a shop. The interior could be distempered or covered with oddments of wall paper. On one of the side walls an imitation fireplace with mantel-shelf could be arranged. A popular item, too, is a dresser fitment consisting of a series of shelves. Those who have the time could make one or two small-size pieces of furniture—say a table and couple of chairs. Give as many realistic touches as possible. Such details as a letter-box, knocker, lock, etc., take little time to fit, and they always appeal to children. Window curtains, preferably to draw, should be provided; also a window-shelf upon which a few flower-pots could be stood.

Generally, these miniature houses are placed against a wall. If this makes the interior somewhat dark, an electric light may be arranged to hang within. Do not have trailing wires on the floor.

TOY ROLLER

THE YOUNGSTER WILL enjoy playing with this indoors or out-of-doors. You can make the roller portion of a size to suit any oddments you may have.

Roller. If you have no suitable round wood (such as an old cornice pole) plane a piece of wood square to the nearest size and mark the circle at the ends. Plain away the corners to form an octagon, and then reduce these corners until the whole approximates to a round. Finish off with a file, giving this a rocking and sideways movement to take out lumps. Follow with glasspaper. Bore holes at the ends in the circle centres to take the pivoting screws.

Handle. To make a really strong job of the handle and other parts a wedged tenon should be cut at top and bottom of the shaft. The corners of the forked portion should be dovetailed. An alternative is to cut out two pieces of strip iron and bend these to shape and screw them to the shaft. Note that washers are inserted between the arms and the roller itself. It is a good plan to paint the latter with a strongly marked design so that the child can easily see it turn round.

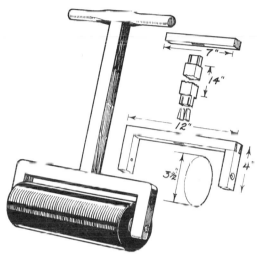

A STRONG TOY TO GIVE ENDLESS FUN

Larger roller. If you want to make a really large roller you can cut out three discs in ⅞ in. wood, say 6 or 9 in. in diameter. These are fixed together by two or more squares of ⅞ in. wood let into notches cut in the diameter. They should be glued and nailed in. Around the whole a sheet of thin plywood is wrapped. The grain should run along the length so that the ply will bend easily. Start at one of the square pieces, allowing the ply to overlap about half-way. Work gradually round, gluing and nailing as you proceed. When you reach the starting place trim the edge if necessary and complete the fixing. Trim the ends when the glue has set. Use screws for pivoting the roller in the same way as in the smaller roller illustration.

BABY WALKER

MANY PARENTS PREFER a low light chair for their child instead of the usual high chair. The low chair is certainly safer as it is practically impossible to overturn, and the child can be kept under better observation. If fitted with rubber-tyred castors as suggested it may be easily wheeled about.

Sizes. The elevation and plan given at Figs. 2 and 4 show a chair roughly 1 ft. 9 in. long by 1 ft. 2 in. wide and 1 ft. 1½ in. high, and if the dimensions given in the details at Figs. 5 to 9 are followed they will result in an article of the above size.

Undercarriage. The undercarriage shown at Fig. 6 is made with two bearers 1 ft. 9 in. long by 2 in. wide by ½ in. thick, joined by screwing or nailing a seat board 1 ft. 2 in. long by 1 ft. wide by

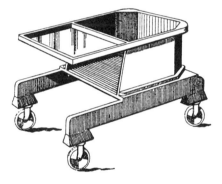

FIG. I. BABY WALKER

½ in. thick to the upper edges, the board being kept 1 in. in from the back ends of the bearers. Before final fixing takes place, however, it will be advisable to fit battens ¾ in. wide by ½ in. thick around the upper side of the seat. The battens are used to hold the sides and back of the chair in place, and the positions for fixing are shown in Fig. 3.

Upper framing. The upper framing (Fig. 5) also carries the sides and back of the chair, and extends forward to form the table. It is made with two side rails 1 ft. 8 in. long by ¾ in. square, joined with a back rail 1 ft. 1 in. long by 3 in. wide, by ¾ in. thick (for exact shaping see Fig. 7), and middle and front rails 1 ft. 1 in. long

120

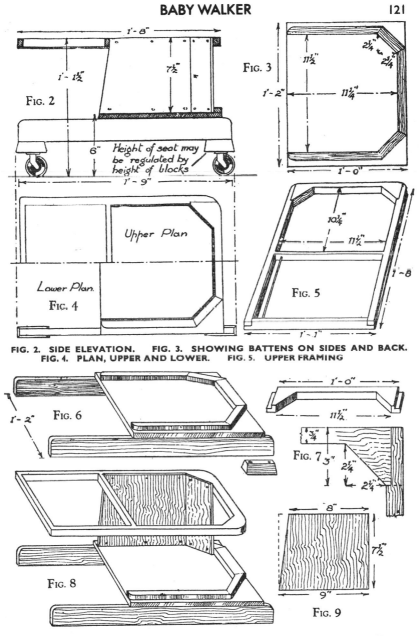

FIG. 2. SIDE ELEVATION.   FIG. 3. SHOWING BATTENS ON SIDES AND BACK.
FIG. 4. PLAN, UPPER AND LOWER.   FIG. 5. UPPER FRAMING

FIG. 6. THE UNDERCARRIAGE.   FIG. 7. CORNER OF UPPER FRAME.
FIG. 8. SKETCH OF FRAMING.   FIG. 9. SHAPE OF SIDES

by $\frac{1}{2}$ in. wide by $\frac{3}{4}$ in. thick. The framing may be half-lapped together and screwed from under the ends of the back rail being recessed $\frac{1}{4}$ in. into the edges of the side rails to avoid sharp corners where it is shaped. Rows of coloured wood play beads could be arranged on one or both sides of the table, or a single row may be carried across at the front. The beads should be on stout wires bored into the framing, and must, of course, be fitted before the joints are finally fixed. A piece of plywood screwed or pinned under the front part of the framing will form the table.

Sides. Thin wood (or plywood) $\frac{1}{4}$ in. thick may be used for the sides and back of the chair. The shape to which the sides should be cut is shown at Fig. 9. They are first screwed to the battens on the seat, and the upper framing may then be placed in position (see Fig. 8), and screws driven through the sides into the framing while at the back and corner pieces are similarly fitted and fixed. The corner joints may be fitted tight, or left open about $\frac{1}{4}$ in. as preferred, the latter being the quicker method. A height from the floor to seat of 6 in. is suggested, but it may be varied. The blocks are 3 in. long by 1 in. high and 1 in. thick, tapered off to meet the bearers and fixed with two screws.

HANDY TRUCK

FOR CARRYING BRICKS or for generally helping in the garden this makes an attractive truck, and it can be made from oddments of timber. Make the main box portion from $\frac{1}{2}$ in. softwood. Trim the ends to size and round over the top edges before assembling. If the sides are made about $\frac{1}{4}$ in. deeper than the ends there will be no complications at the joints. Put the parts together with glue and nails, using resin preferably as it is highly water-resistant. Punch in the nails and fill the holes. For the bottom $\frac{3}{8}$ in. or $\frac{1}{2}$ in. plywood is advisable. Glue and nail from beneath.

An axle tree is screwed on beneath. In the middle of it is a notch to take the end of the rear support (see sketch). The wheels, which can be cut in solid wood or ply, are pivoted on round-head screws with washers at both sides.

The rear shaft is tenoned at the top into the handle, being taken right through and wedged. Note how the handle ends are rounded over with chisel and finished with glasspaper. At the lower end a piece is planted on at each side to form a fork. This enables it to be held to the support with bolts and thumbscrews.

Finish the whole thing with oil paint both inside and out. Note that, as the wheel screws are entering end grain, they cannot have maximum strength. They should therefore be as long as possible, and the axle tree itself should be in hardwood.

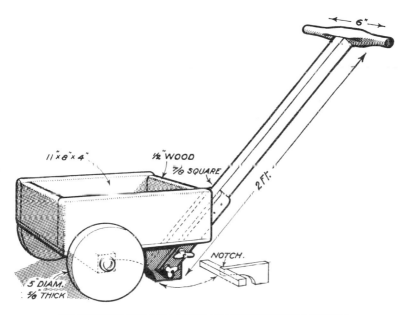

11″×8″×4″   ½″ WOOD   ⅞ SQUARE   2 FT.   6″   NOTCH.   5 DIAM.   ⅝ THICK

THE YOUNGSTER WILL ENJOY CARRYING THINGS IN THIS

SEE-SAW BOAT

THIS IS A simple toy that will keep the youngsters amused for hours in the garden. It is provided with a pair of rockers and a seat at each end, and a couple of children can rock themselves up and down just as in a real boat. There is no bottom, but just a cross board (D) to form a foot rest. The whole thing is easily made from deal battens and plywood.

Sides. The two plywood sides ($\frac{3}{16}$ in.) are 4 ft. 4 in. long by 1 ft.

FIG. I. AN EXCELLENT TOY FOR INDOORS OR GARDEN

8 in. wide. To mark out the sloping sides measure in a distance of 3 in. along the bottom edge at both ends and draw in pencil lines to the top corners. The curve is struck by marking up $5\frac{3}{4}$ in. and bending a lath to run through these points to strike the bottom edge at the centre. The top shape is 4 in. down. All these details are given in Fig. 2. The shape can be cut out with the bow saw.

Rockers. The two rockers (A) are about 4 ft. 1 in. long by $8\frac{3}{4}$ in. wide by $\frac{7}{8}$ in. thick. They are placed in position against the plywood to enable the shape to be transferred. They are nailed to the inside of the ply. For the uprights (B), $\frac{5}{8}$ in. stuff can be used. They can cut economically from the board by marking a line more or less diagonally. They are nailed to the outside of the ply. Several long stout nails should be driven right through where the uprights (B) cross the rockers (A), and be clenched inside. There are two top rails (C) and here again nails are driven through and clenched. Before they are put on, however, two holes should be bored in each to hold the handles. After all nails have been driven in the edges can be levelled all round.

Footboard. The footboard (D), the two seats (E), and the end rails (F) are prepared next. Nail the footboard right through the rockers, and place the seats on the top edge of the latter. The end

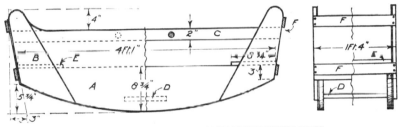

FIG. 2. SIDE AND END ELEVATIONS WITH SIZES

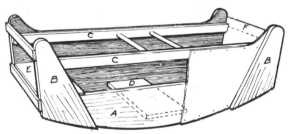

FIG. 3. HOW PARTS
ARE PUT TOGETHER

CUTTING LIST

					Long ft.	in.	Wide in.	Thick in.
(A)	2	Rockers	..	..	4	2	9	$\frac{7}{8}$
(B)	4	Uprights	..	..	1	10	8	$\frac{5}{8}$
(C)	2	Rails	..	..	4	4	$2\frac{1}{4}$	$\frac{5}{8}$
(D)	1	Footboard	..	..	1	$1\frac{1}{2}$	8	$\frac{7}{8}$
(E)	2	Seats	..	..	1	$3\frac{1}{2}$	9	$\frac{5}{8}$
(F)	4	Rails	..	..	1	5	$2\frac{1}{4}$	$\frac{3}{8}$
	2	Panels	..	..	4	4	20	$\frac{3}{16}$ ply
	2	Handles	..	..	1	5		1 dowel rod

rails (F) are screwed on after the end panels have been nailed on. In Fig. 3 the panels are omitted for clearness. The handles are 1 in. dowel rods, and they must be inserted in their holes before seats or footboard are fixed. The whole thing is finished with a couple of coats of paint.

As in all toys for children the edges and corners should be rounded over with glasspaper.

PENGUIN TIC-TAC-TOE

THIS LITTLE GAME will give fun to the young (and probably to the older folk as well!). The aim is to get three penguins in a row either across, down, or diagonally before your opponent does. You

FIG. 1. THE GAME IS PLAYED SIMILARLY TO NOUGHTS AND CROSSES

need ten penguins—five for each player and the first player to get three in a row is declared the winner.

There is, of course, no actual construction. You will need a piece of $\frac{5}{8}$ in. thick plywood, $7\frac{1}{4}$ in. square. This is subdivided into nine squares (shown in Fig. 2) and the top edges should be well rounded. The dividing lines are V-shaped grooves cut into the block about $\frac{1}{16}$ in. wide by $\frac{1}{16}$ in. deep and here a parting (or vee) tool is invaluable. In the centre of each square a countersunk hole is drilled to a depth of

$\frac{3}{8}$ in. to take the $\frac{3}{8}$ in. diameter dowel-peg which is fixed to the foot of the penguin.

The illustration of the penguin in Fig. 3 is actual size, so that you can mark out from it. It is of $\frac{1}{8}$ in. thick ply inserted into a slot cut into a piece of $\frac{3}{8}$ in. dowel, glued and tapered off as in Fig. 3. An easy way to handle these short pieces is to get a length of $\frac{3}{8}$ in. dowel about 6 in. longer than the actual required length. Slot and taper it off whilst it is held in a vice, then cut off the required length; repeat the process until you have ten pieces.

As already mentioned, ten penguins are needed, five coloured in black and five coloured in light grey. The cross-shaded areas on the beak and feet are orange colour in both cases. The penguins are, of course, painted both sides.

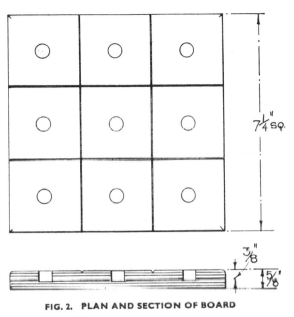

FIG. 2. PLAN AND SECTION OF BOARD

FIG. 3. FULL SIZE DETAIL OF PENGUIN
You can trace over this to get a correct outline. The cross-shaded areas are coloured orange

DOLL'S CRIB

A STURDY, SIMPLY-DESIGNED toy which will give hours of pleasure.

Joints throughout are mortise and tenon and present no difficulty. The drop-side rails (C) can be grooved throughout their length to take the tenons on the slats. Ply panels (D) are pinned and glued to

FIG. I. TOY TO PLEASE A GIRL

the outside of the end framing, part B being shaped after the framing has been assembled, but before the ply is glued on. The drop-side rails (C) are also grooved at each end (Fig. 2) to slide up and down a bead fixed to A. Fig. 3 shows the method employed to operate the sliding drop-side, and either one or both sides can be made to drop, the block being fixed to either the outside as shown, or the inside.

The "mattress" could be either upholsterer's webbing, or even rubber webbing. If the latter is used, do not strain it too tightly, or the frame will be distorted.

Colour lacquer or gloss paint could be used as a finish, with decorative transfers.

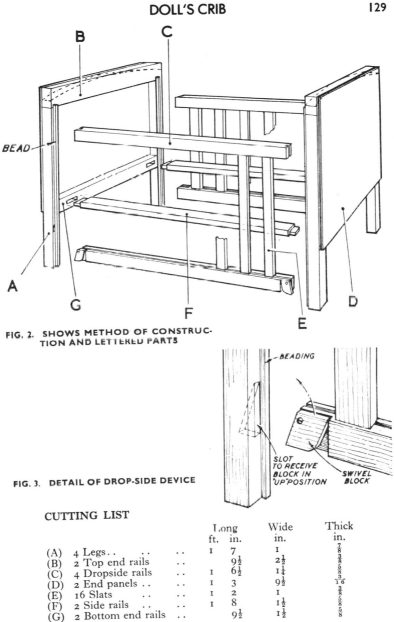

FIG. 2. SHOWS METHOD OF CONSTRUCTION AND LETTERED PARTS

BEAD

FIG. 3. DETAIL OF DROP-SIDE DEVICE

BEADING

SLOT
TO RECEIVE
BLOCK IN
"UP"POSITION

SWIVEL
BLOCK

CUTTING LIST

			Long ft.	Long in.	Wide in.	Thick in.
(A)	4 Legs..	..	1	7	1	$\frac{7}{8}$
(B)	2 Top end rails	..		$9\frac{1}{2}$	$2\frac{1}{2}$	$\frac{3}{8}$
(C)	4 Dropside rails	..	1	$6\frac{1}{2}$	$1\frac{1}{4}$	$\frac{5}{8}$
(D)	2 End panels ..	..	1	3	$9\frac{1}{2}$	$\frac{3}{16}$
(E)	16 Slats	..	1	2	1	$\frac{3}{8}$
(F)	2 Side rails	..	1	8	$1\frac{1}{2}$	$\frac{5}{8}$
(G)	2 Bottom end rails	..		$9\frac{1}{2}$	$1\frac{1}{2}$	$\frac{5}{8}$

Blocks from odd stuff.
Allowances have been made to lengths and widths.
Thicknesses are net.

HORSE ON WHEELS

APART FROM THE fun the child gets out of this, it will prove extremely useful when you want to take him a little way along the road to do some shopping or to post a letter. It will give him a definite incentive to go out and will save a lot of unwilling dragging along the road.

Body. This is cut out of a solid block and could be of any suitable

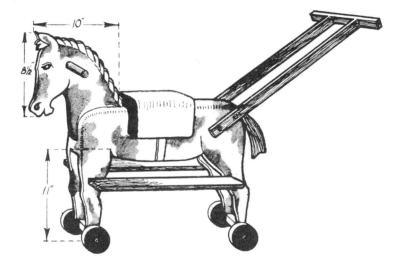

FIG. I. A HORSE ON WHICH THE YOUNGSTER CAN RIDE
The child for whom this was made enjoyed every minute spent with it. Useful additions for the younger child are footboards and a bar for the hands

thickness. That shown was $3\frac{1}{2}$ in. Notches have to be cut in it to hold the legs and the head, and the marking out and cutting of these is the next job. They can be partly sawn and partly chiselled (see Fig. 3). A hole for the tail is also needed at the rear, and this can be bored at a suitable angle to hold an old brush. Round over all edges and corners when the joints are complete.

Head and legs. These could be in $\frac{7}{8}$ in. or 1 in. wood. Taking first the head, sketch the shape and saw out with bow or keyhole saw. A most realistic shape can be obtained by cutting in the eyes and nostrils with a gouge. The mane, too, can be thinned down and carved with the gouge in resemblance of hair. Glue the head in its notch and drive in one or two skew nails.

Cut out the legs in a similar way and plane the top ends square. Slightly bevel the insides so that they splay outwards, and trim the edges at a corresponding angle. Round over all edges, using file or spokeshave, finishing off with glasspaper. Fix with glue and deeply recessed screws, and fill in the holes with dowels. These details are shown in Fig. 2. Cross bars at the feet are not essential, but they add to the rigidity, and also give a bearing for extra long screws for the wheels.

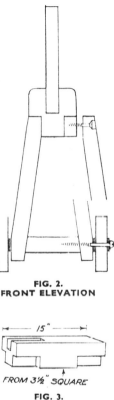

FIG. 2.
FRONT ELEVATION

For the last named either cut out discs in $\frac{3}{4}$ in. wood or use metal disc wheels. Washers are desirable on both sides. An alternative is to use metal axles with holes drilled through to take lynch pins. These with washers at the sides keep the wheels in position. Handles can be made of two $\frac{1}{2}$ in. strips 1 in. wide screwed to the hind quarters and wedge-tenoned to the cross piece (see Fig. 1). A handle that the child can grip can be rounded in section and passed through a hole bored right through the neck. Footboards too are desirable. These should extend from front to back legs and be fixed with screws. Slightly canting the inner edges will enable them to lie horizontally.

15"

FROM 3½" SQUARE

FIG. 3.
HOW BODY IS MADE

It will be realised that the success of this toy depends largely upon the painting. Prepare the surface thoroughly first, rounding over all corners and edges, and filling in any nail holes and other blemishes with plastic wood. The legs, head, and so on should be well rounded, a spokeshave and file being used. Finish off with glasspaper—middle 2 grade is the most suitable. The colours can be in any natural colours—white and black, grey, bay and white, etc. Handles and wheels can be black. These should be removed before painting begins. Begin with priming followed by a flat coat and finish off with a glossy paint.

The child for whom this horse was made was about two years old, and the sizes were just right. It suited him until well over three. There is no need to keep rigidly to them, however. It may be necessary to adapt them in accordance with the wood available. Other animals, too, could be made.

It is obviously necessary for the wheels to be thoroughly strong and securely pivoted. Use long and thick round-head screws. Drive them in until the heads are just short of binding on the washers. The wheels should be free to revolve easily, but not unduly slack because this gives side play which tends to produce wobbling.

DUMP TRUCK

THE CHASSIS (A) IS the main section of the truck to which the cab and body are fitted. The cab is constructed by fixing the seat to the back (B) and fastening the latter to the chassis. The back edge of B should fit flush with the shoulders on the chassis, marked (C).

The engine block (D) is fitted to the chassis and strengthens the front of the cab. The dashboard (E) forms the shape of the front, and the front (F) and sides (G) are fixed to it. The whole is fixed to the engine block. The sides (H) fit into the recessed sides of the

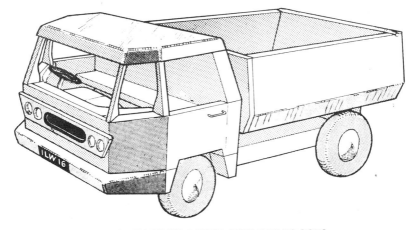

FIG. 1. THIS WILL APPEAL SPECIALLY TO BOYS

Length is about 12 in. and width 7 in., but dimensions could be varied within a little as required

back (B), and can be fixed to the end of the seat for added rigidity. Piece (G) fits behind the front.

The roof (J) is fixed down temporarily to enable the shaping and fitting of its supports (K), the tops of which are shaped to a dowel on

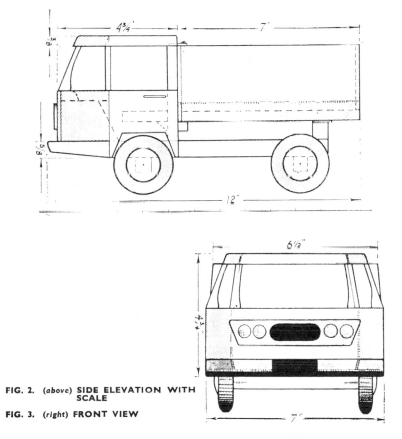

FIG. 2. *(above)* **SIDE ELEVATION WITH SCALE**

FIG. 3. *(right)* **FRONT VIEW**

the back edge, as can be seen in Fig. 3.   Holes of the equivalent size are drilled into the underside of the roof to accommodate them.   The bottom ends are pinned down to the dashboard.   These should be quite steady and well fixed to give support to the front of the roof.

The radiator and headlamps are incorporated in one piece (L). The lamps are drill holes, and a groove is cut or a shape painted on to indicate the radiator grid.   It should be noted that the underside of the chassis tapers at the front to form the bumpers, to which a number plate is added.

The body consists of the base (M), two edges of which are tapered in slightly to give the slope of the sides (N). The bottom edge of the sides should be shaped before fixing to the base. The end piece (O) is fixed to the ends of the base and sides. The back edge of the body (P) fits inside the side pieces (N). A piece of dowel is fixed on the top edge, with $\frac{1}{4}$ in. protruding at each end to engage in the groove cut in the sides. When the body is tipped up the back will automatically swing open for unloading. A strip of wood is fixed to the back of the cab, upon which the body rests, as can be seen in Fig. 2. Another strip of wood (Q) is hinged to the underside of the base and fixed to the chassis. This gives the tipping action. Two small

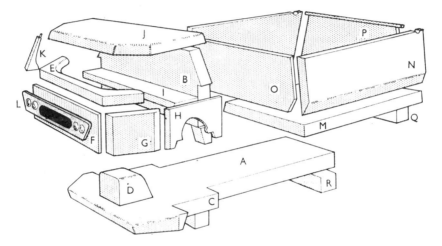

FIG. 4. HOW THE PARTS FIT TOGETHER

turnbuttons are fitted to the sides to engage in slots cut into the back of the cab, so securing the body when it is not being used for tipping.

Two strips of wood are fitted to the underside of the chassis to which the wheels are fitted. All parts are glued and pinned or screwed as necessary.

Pieces F, H, L, O, P, are of thin plywood. The remainder of the sections are of softwood. The thickness varies according to the section being made.

THE TOY SHOP

CHILDREN DELIGHT IN playing at "shops", deriving a great amount of amusement from it, and the toy shown at Fig. 1 is one of the best presents the woodworker could make for a child. The

FIG. I. TOY SHOP 20 in. by 15 in. OVER BASE

construction is most interesting and gives scope for much ingenuity, and by the use of plywood the cost may be kept quite low. In this model the shop occupies the whole of the ground floor, and there are two rooms on the first floor. The premises may be fitted up for any sort of trade, or by the provision of suitable fittings in the way of portable counters and shelves, and with the necessary stock the toy

135

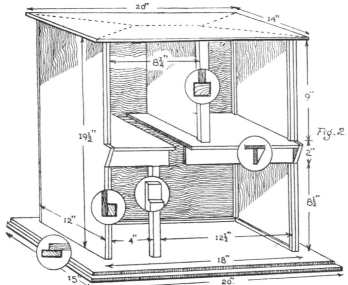

FIG. 2. MAIN SIZES AND CONSTRUCTION DETAILS

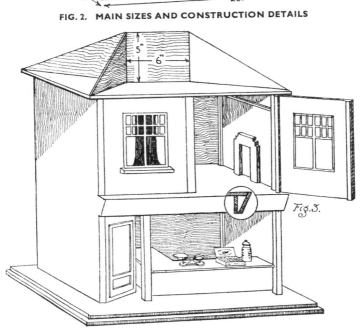

FIG. 3. GENERAL VIEW SHOWING ROOF SUPPORTS

will prove of much more interest. Small pieces may be carved from scraps of wood and painted to represent boxes, loaves, cakes, etc., while small bottles may be purchased for a confectionery business. Joints may be made by the same means for a butchery, and miniature tables and chairs would set up a tea-shop.

The main construction is clearly shown in Fig. 2, and although sizes are given they may be amended to suit any special requirements. Be sure of good proportions. Plywood of $\frac{3}{16}$ in. or $\frac{1}{4}$ in. thickness may be used, although it should be strengthened where necessary with small fillets. The ends are 1 ft. 7$\frac{1}{2}$ in. high by 11$\frac{3}{4}$ in. wide, fillets $\frac{1}{2}$ in. wide by $\frac{1}{4}$ in. thick being nailed at all the edges. The top is 1 ft. 8 in. long by 1 ft. 2 in. wide, nailed down to the ends to overhang 1 in. all round, and the bottom 1 ft. 8 in. long by 1 ft. 3 in. wide is nailed to overhang 1 in. at the ends and back, and 2 in. at the front. Fillets $\frac{3}{4}$ in. wide by $\frac{1}{4}$ in. thick are used to thicken the edges of the bottom. They are mitred at the corners, and overhang $\frac{1}{4}$ in. The floor is roughly 1 ft. 5$\frac{5}{8}$ in. long by 1 ft. 0$\frac{1}{2}$ in. wide. This width permits it to overhang the ends $\frac{3}{4}$ in. at the front. Fillets should be nailed across the ends for support, and it is nailed in place. A piece of wood 1 ft. 7$\frac{1}{2}$ in. by 1 ft. 6 in. is used to cover in the back. Two small shaped triangular pieces 2 in. long by $\frac{3}{4}$ in. wide at the top are fixed to the front edges of the ends level with the floor, and a strip 1$\frac{3}{4}$ in. wide is fixed across underneath the floor, level, with the edges of the ends, the fillets being cut away for its reception. The doorway of the shop is formed by fitting an upright $\frac{1}{2}$ in. square. It runs up behind the strip under the floor to stand level at the front, and is glued and nailed. A division of plywood is fitted midway across the floor to form the two rooms, and a $\frac{1}{2}$ in. upright is fixed at the front edge. The shop fascia is completed by nailing a strip of wood across the edges of the floor and triangular pieces, as shown in Fig. 3.

The fronts (Fig. 4) of the rooms are 9 in. by 8$\frac{1}{4}$ in., strengthened at the edges with $\frac{1}{2}$ in. by $\frac{1}{4}$ in. fillets, and pierced with an opening 5 in. by 4 in. Fretwood of $\frac{1}{8}$ in. thickness should be used to cut the overlaid window frame (Fig. 5), which is 5$\frac{1}{4}$ in. by 4$\frac{1}{4}$ in. over all, with the main parts $\frac{1}{4}$ in. wide and the rest $\frac{1}{8}$ in. The frame is glued outside the opening to form rebates for the glass which is held with fillets, while a sill is fixed outside. Small hinges are used to hinge the fronts to the ends, and buttons are fitted for fastening. The shop door (Fig. 6) is 8$\frac{1}{2}$ in. by 4 in., pierced with an opening 5 in. by 3 in.; an overlay (Fig. 7) is glued outside, and glass is fitted, while the completed door is hinged on the left-hand side. Modern mantelpieces (Fig. 8) could be fitted in the rooms, the upright members being 2$\frac{1}{2}$ in. long by $\frac{3}{4}$ in. wide by $\frac{1}{2}$ in. thick, and the top 4 in. long

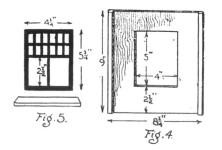

Fig. 5.

Fig. 4.

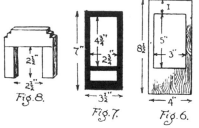

Fig. 8.

Fig. 7.

Fig. 6.

FIG. 4. UPPER FRONT
FIG. 5. WINDOW FRAME
FIG. 6. DOOR
FIG. 7. DOOR OVERLAY
FIG. 8. MANTELPIECE

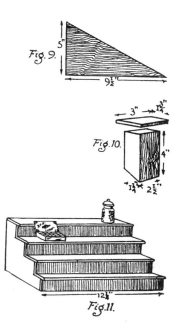

Fig. 9.

Fig. 10.

Fig. 11.

FIG. 9. ROOF SUPPORT
FIG. 10. CHIMNEY
FIG. 11. DISPLAY STAND

by 1 in. wide with the ends shaped as shown. Small slips of wood chamfered at the bottom edge would form picture rails.

The roof is built up as shown at Fig. 3, the ridge piece being 6 in. long by 5 in. high nailed through the top, while four shaped rafter pieces (Fig. 9) run from it to the corners. Plywood jointed over the rafters and nailed down is used to cover the roof. Chimneys (Fig. 10) fixed at each end of the roof are very effective. They are made with a shaft 4 in. long by $2\frac{1}{2}$ in. wide by $1\frac{1}{4}$ in. thick, having the bottom end cut to the slope of the roof, and completed with a thin capping 3 in. by $1\frac{3}{4}$ in.

The shop could be fitted up with shelves at the back and end. It is inadvisable to enclose the front with glass, but a portable counter made L-shape to run across the front and towards the back is excellent. A set of stages or sloping shelves (Fig. 11) which may be substituted in its place offers a change in dressing, and will hold the interest of a child.

Doll's house paper could be used to finish the top. The walls of the rooms should be papered.

HOBBY HORSE

Construction of this is obvious from the diagrams. The head can be fretted out of plywood or solid wood about $\frac{3}{4}$ in. thick. It is fixed with screws to the main shaft. The latter is about $1\frac{1}{4}$ in. wide at the wheel end, and tapers to 1 in. at the head. It is through-tenoned and wedged to the axle tree, and struts are added at each side, being

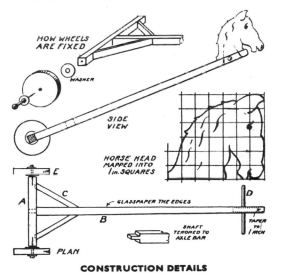

CONSTRUCTION DETAILS

notched in and glued and nailed. The wheels are pivoted on round-head screws with washers at each side.

FIG. 1. MECHANICAL TOY THAT GIVES ENDLESS FUN
The movement is imparted to the boats by bevel gearing

THE MOVEMENT OF the merry-go-round is arranged by means of bevel gearing. These gears can be obtained in brass in various sizes. Model-making shops frequently stock them, and miscellaneous disposal shops often have them for sale. The exact size is not important, but it is advisable to obtain them first so that the sizes of the parts can be made to suit. The large gear wheel is fitted to the bottom end of the main spindle A. To keep the spindle upright a cross piece F is fixed to the base D and a hole cut in it to receive the bottom gear wheel. To steady it at the top a collar piece P is arranged in two parts to engage a groove turned in the spindle A. In this way the collar pieces can be added after the spindle is erected in position.

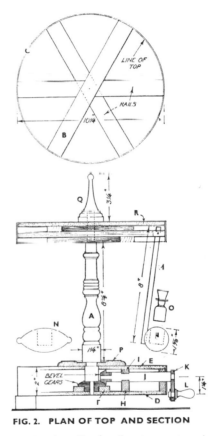

FIG. 2. PLAN OF TOP AND SECTION

The small spindle J to which the handle is fixed rotates in a hole in the piece G, and at the inside fits in the bearing engaging in the turned slot. This bearing is in two parts, H, and top piece I which is screwed on afterwards. The position of the bearing is found by adjusting it back and forth so that the correct engagement of the bevel gears is found.

At the top is a disc supported by three rails B (see Fig. 3). These are fitted one above the other, and blocks are therefore necessary on two of them to make a flush surface at the upper side on which the

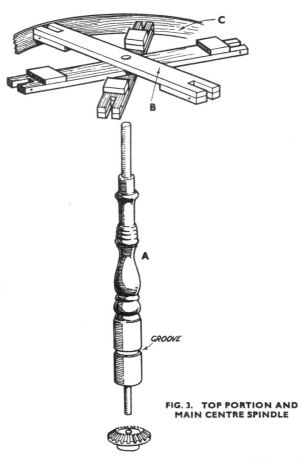

FIG. 3. TOP PORTION AND MAIN CENTRE SPINDLE

disc can rest. The spindle A passes through a hole which is bored through the three cross bars. The ends of the last named are slotted at the ends to enable the arms to be pivoted. To the ends of the arms are fixed the boats N, which in turn hold the turned dolls O. The last named are left loose.

Spindle. As the size to which this is turned is dependent upon the bevel gears, it is necessary to obtain the last named first. The exact design is not important, but it is a good plan to introduce plenty of small members as these look very well when painted in bright colours. Turn the bottom end to fit the hole in the bevel gear, and form a long $\frac{1}{2}$ in. dowel at the top to pass through the rails B and into the turned finial Q. Also put in the groove near the bottom to take the collar piece P. It is a good idea to draw out a section of the working parts in full size so that the exact position of the members can be ascertained. The bevel gear is additionally held by long thin screws. It may be necessary to drill holes in the wheel to take them.

Top disc. Cut all three rails B to the same length, and glue them together as in Fig. 2 so that they are spaced at 60 deg. Bore a hole through the middle to take the dowel, and to the ends of the top one glue on pieces of the same thickness at the underside. To the bottom

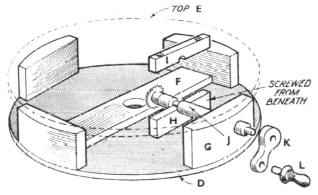

FIG. 4. LOWER PORTION SHOWING MECHANISM

one glue on similar pieces but on the top. These are to enable the arms M to be pivoted from the same level. Cut ⅜ in. slots at all six ends to take the arms, and drill through at the sides to allow little pieces of $\frac{1}{16}$ in. wire to be passed through as in Fig. 2.

As the top disc R has to lie flat on the rails it is necessary to put packing pieces on four of the ends (Fig. 3). Glue on the disc R, driving a pin into the end of each rail. Level the ends of the rails with the disc and add the edging C. This could be in thin ply, or in a good bending wood such as beech. Make the joint opposite one of the arms. Boring the hole through the disc completes this part of the work, except for the top finial Q which, however, is added later.

Base mechanism. Cut out the top and bottom discs E and D to finish 10¼ in. Hardboard is suitable. To it glue and nail the four pieces G as in Fig. 4, levelling outer edges to the disc. One has a hole bored through it to take the small spindle J. At right angles to the spindle fix the cross piece F, this having a hole in it to take the bevel gear. The small spindle J is turned as in Figs. 2 and 4, and once the correct position for the engagement of the bevel gears is found the bottom bearing piece H can be fixed with screws from underneath. The addition of the top piece I prevents movement back and forth. In making these parts the two should be screwed together and the hole bored through the joint. They are then separated.

The crank K is glued and pinned, and handle L passes freely through its hole and is held by a cotter-pin. When all is in order place the vertical spindle A in position and fix the top with screws. The addition of the collar pieces P (fixed with screws) enables the action to be tried.

Cardboard is used around the outer surface. Glue and pin it, arranging the joint opposite the handle spindle. Finally make a neat finish by sticking gummed tape all round the top edge. The base blocks are screwed on from underneath.

Boats. These are turned between centres and parted off. The large holes to take the dolls are also worked on the lathe. A special form of cradle is set up on the face plate to hold the boat, and the hole is turned out with ordinary turning tools. A notch is filed across one side, and the arm M glued and screwed. At the top of the arm is a small hole to hold the pivoting wire. The dolls can be turned to various shapes.

Finishing. Flat oil paints can be used if preferred, this being followed by a coat of copal varnish. A rather more manageable method, however, is to use poster water colours which cover well. Various colours can be used, and the faces of the dolls can be put in. This is followed by either copal varnish or clear cellulose.

CUTTING LIST

			Long ft.	Long in.	Wide in.	Thick in.
A	1	Spindle	1	2	1½ square	—
B	3	Rails		10½	1¼	⅜
C	1	Edging	3	0	1⅝	3/32
D	1	Base		10½	10½	¼
E	1	Top		10½	10½	¼
F	1	Cross piece		10	2⅝	⅜
G	4	Blocks		1	1⅝	⅞
H, I	1	Bearing		3¼	1¾	½
J	1	Spindle		5½	⅞ square	—
K	1	Crank		2½	¾	¼
L	1	Handle		2½	⅞	—
M	6	Rods		8½	5/16	—
N	6	Boats		5¼	2 square	—
O	6	Dolls		3	1 square	—
P	1	Retaining ring		5	5	⅜
Q	1	Finial		4	2 square	—
R	1	Top		10½	10½	¼

Items D, E and R can be in hardboard.

Allowance has been made in lengths and widths. Thicknesses are net. Turned items allow for chucking and turning, but sizes can be adapted to suit method used. When a lathe is not available construction should be adapted, and sizes altered accordingly.

TABLE TENNIS TOP
Made in chipboard

THE GENERALLY RECOGNISED size for a table tennis top for tournament play is 9 ft. by 5 ft., but, as a rule, this is too big for use in the small house. A top of 8 ft. by 4 ft. is the largest that can be used, and even this is usually made in two parts jointed together in the middle to enable it to be stored away when not in use.

The main tops are in chipboard ½ in. thick, which gives perfectly good play for home use. A rebated edging is mitred all round, this helping to stiffen the whole thing and giving a neat finish all round.

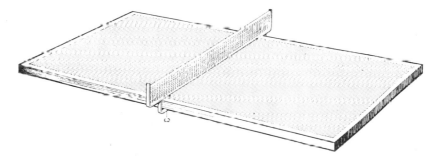

FIG. I. TABLE TENNIS TOP. IDEAL FOR HOME USE
For convenience in storing the top is made in two with centre joint. Size is 8 ft. by 4 ft.

As the top in Fig. 1 is 8 ft. by 4 ft. it is made in two pieces, partly to enable it to be stored conveniently when not in use, and partly to cut down the weight to be lifted. Those who have the space could, of course, leave the board in a single piece. It is intended to rest upon an ordinary dining table, and if this opens out to the usual 5 ft. length there is ample support. Chipboard is normally straight and flat, but is of considerable weight. Consequently when laid down flat there is inevitable sagging. This means that a stiffening edging or framework is needed. Apart from helping to keep the whole thing flat it protects the edges of the chipboard and conceals them.

Chipboard panels. The board in Fig. 1 has an edging of 1½ in by ⅞ in. stuff, this being rebated at the top. It is glued, and screws are driven upwards through it into the chipboard. The corners are

145

mitred and are strengthened with angle brackets glued and screwed in. These stand away from the top by about $\frac{1}{8}$ in. so that they do not affect the resiliency. For the same reason the intermediate cross-rail fitted between the edging of each section is slightly curved in length so that it does not actually touch the underside of the top. If it were to do so there might be a slightly different bounce to the ball locally.

Plimber chipboard is 8 ft. by 4 ft. by $\frac{1}{2}$ in., and it is necessary to cross-cut it at the middle to make two 4 ft. square panels. In case there is any tendency to curvature it is advisable to arrange the two pieces so that they are in the same relative position when the table is in use. Put a pencil identification mark to make sure of it The cross-cut saw can be used for cutting, after which the sawn edge should be trimmed straight and square. You will find it a little hard on the edge of your plane, but there is not a lot of planing to be done. It is as well to go over the remaining three edges of each piece as a clean joint is needed for the edging.

Edging. A section through this is given in Fig. 3. The stuff is $1\frac{1}{2}$ in. by $\frac{7}{8}$ in. and a $\frac{1}{2}$ in. rebate is worked at the top edge to take the chipboard. Those having access to a circular saw can work the rebate easily in two cuts, one with the wood on edge and the other on

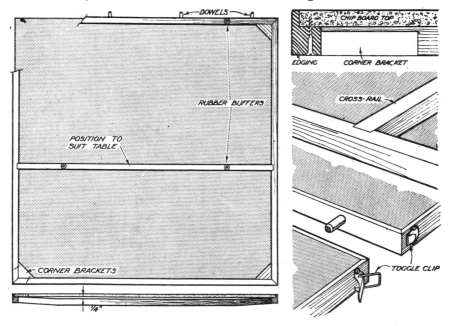

FIG. 2. UNDERSIDE SHOWING CROSS-RAIL　　**FIG. 3. CONSTRUCTION DETAILS**

its side.   Failing this the filister plane will have to be used—or a fence can be fixed temporarily to the rebate plane.

The corners are mitred, and wood angle brackets are glued and screwed in to strengthen them.   This, however, is best done after the edgings have been glued and screwed.   The simplest plan is to plane the brackets to fit, glue them, and rub them in position. Screws are driven in after the glue has set.   If this is not done the mitre may be forced open by pressure of the screws as the last named are tightened.   The brackets are $\frac{3}{4}$ in. thick and are fixed flush at the underside so leaving a slight gap beneath the chip board.

The best way of dealing with the edgings is to cut the mitres of one piece, trim to an exact fit, and glue in position.   Three thumb-screws will hold it in position.   Screws are then driven in straight-way and the thumb-screws removed.   (The screw holes must, of course, be bored and countersunk beforehand.)   Now add the adjacent edging and fix in the same way, and work similarly all round.

One detail to be noted is that the side edgings need small notches cut across them to take the cross-rail.   In some cases the position can be central, but generally it is better to off-set it towards the outer edge because this gives a definite tendency for the centre to drop on to the table.   Without this the ends may sag downwards.   It is better to cut the notches before the side edgings are fixed.

Cross-rail.   Details of this are given in Fig. 2.   It is $1\frac{1}{4}$ in. by $\frac{7}{8}$ in. section, and the top edge is cut down $\frac{1}{4}$ in. as shown.   Gauge a line $\frac{1}{4}$ in. from the top edge, and 9 in. from each end draw a straight line to reach to the top corner.   The waste can be either sawn or planed away.   A corresponding sloping line is drawn at the underside. Glue in the notches and drive a skew nail into each joint.

To ensure that the two boards are level when put together, four dowels are let into the edge of one and corresponding holes bored in the other (see Fig. 2).   To hold them together during play a toggle clip is fitted at each side, as in Fig. 3.   The addition of rubber buffers, such as are used for W.C. seats, to the underside of the framework completes the job.   They should be positioned to suit the table on which the top is to rest.   One point to note is that many table extensions sag and this may mean that some of the buffers may have to be packed up.   The only plan is to test the top on the actual table.

Painting.   Before the war it was possible to obtain a finish made specially for the purpose.   This is practically impossible to-day, and the only plan is to use one coat of grey priming paint followed by one of dark green undercoating.   This dries flat without shine.   A refinement is to paint a $\frac{3}{4}$ in. white margin all round.

DOLL'S HOUSE

A SIZE OF 3 ft. 2 in. by 1 ft. 6 in. over the base is convenient in most cases, but if lack of space is a difficulty the garage could be omitted and the base cut down to 2 ft. 6 in. by 1 ft. 6 in.

It will be seen that the left-hand front opens at a point level with the right-hand front, so that the whole bay and a portion of the room opens with it. At the right-hand side the front opens level with the inner wall of the balcony. Both these details are shown in Fig. 2. One of the roofs can be made to hinge, or a flap can be cut in it to allow batteries to be inserted by those who wish to electrify the rooms. If this is done it is as well to arrange all the wiring during construction as it is then much easier to insert it.

Main walls. The construction depends largely upon the material available. As plywood may be difficult to obtain, a good plan is to use hardboard such as *Masonite*, or plastic board. As this has little

FIG. 1   REALISTIC HOUSE WITH FOUR ROOMS AND GARAGE
Size over base is 3 ft. 2 in. by 1 ft. 6 in.

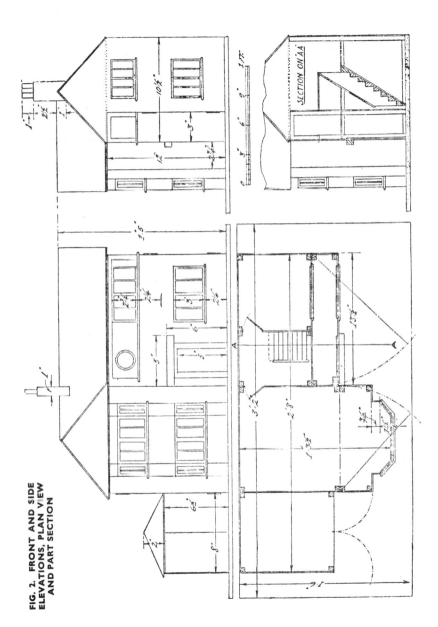

FIG. 2. FRONT AND SIDE ELEVATIONS, PLAN VIEW AND PART SECTION

stiffness in itself it is necessary to put in corner strips to which it can be glued and nailed. In the same way floors should rest upon strips or battens as it is impossible to drive nails into the edges.

Begin with the back which can be in a single sheet including the garage. Square upon it the positions of the walls, and from it mark the sizes of the fronts. The floors can also be marked in. Next cut out the three front-to-back walls (the garage can follow afterwards). All three are the same depth because, although the right-hand wall reaches only to the back of the balcony, it has to fill in the space beneath the roof (see side view in Fig. 2). This right-hand wall is taller than the others because it has to extend to the ridge whilst the others terminate beneath the eaves. Mark on each the floor positions, and any windows and doors. The openings can be cut with the fretsaw. If neatly done no trimming will be required.

Corner strips and battens are glued and nailed to these walls, and, the glue having set, they can be added to the back. Always drive the nails through the fibre board into the solid wood. The ceilings of the ground floor can be cut out, and it should be noted that in the hall it has to be cut away for the staircase. Again fix with glue and nails. At the top it is advisable to fix down a single ceiling over the whole. This will have to jut forward to fill in the space above the opening fronts which include the balcony and the bay. The over-hanging roofs can rest upon this ceiling and there is thus no danger of their fouling the fronts when these are opened.

Base. This can be either a single sheet of stout plywood or chipboard, or it can be a piece of hardboard mounted on wide solid battens. In the latter case the simplest way is to mitre the battens at the corners and glue and nail the hardboard to them. Intermediate cross-battens can be arranged wherever stiffening seems desirable; for instance, beneath the front-to-back walls. This will enable the strips at the bottom of the walls to be nailed down. When chipboard is used there is no difficulty; the strips can be nailed straight down.

Roof. To provide a suitable surface to which the roofs can be fixed it is necessary to add triangular pieces as in Fig. 5. That at the right-hand end already exists as a continuation of the wall, and all that is required is to add strips into which nails can be driven. The method of finding the shape of the roof panels appears in Fig. 4. Take the left-hand roof. The length at ridge is known ($10\frac{1}{2}$ in.), also that at eaves (16 in.), and the width can be taken from the elevation ($7\frac{3}{4}$ in.). If these sizes are drawn in on the sheet of fibre board the angle at the hip follows automatically. The parts should be mitred where they meet, and it is a good plan to stick a piece of

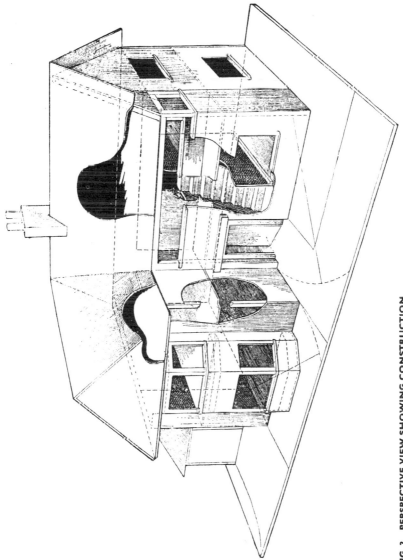

FIG. 3 PERSPECTIVE VIEW SHOWING CONSTRUCTION

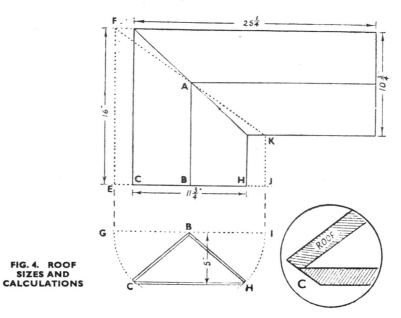

**FIG. 4. ROOF
SIZES AND
CALCULATIONS**

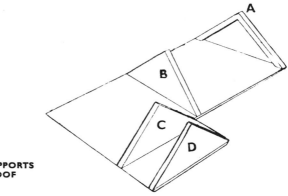

**FIG. 5. SUPPORTS
FOR ROOF**

gummed tape along the joints. This gives a neat finish and helps to resemble the ridge tiles. A panel can be cut in, say, the large back roof to give access to the loft to enable batteries to be stored. It can be hinged with a strip of fine canvas glued on.

Both the bay and the balcony front can be made up complete. Note from the dotted lines in Fig. 3 how a solid block is inserted in the bay at both top and bottom. This enables the wall and window pieces to be glued and nailed on. The window openings are cut to the glass size, and separate frames in thin wood or in plastic board are pinned on at the front. The openings in these are made smaller so that a rebate is formed in which the glass can fit. The glasses are held either with small nails at the back or with little strips of gummed tape.

Details can be added as desired. Doors can be hinged with small brass butts or with canvas glued on. The staircase consists of a flat board with triangular strips glued on, and with a side glued on to form the panelled balustrade. The whole thing can be finished with paint, or doll's house brick paper and tiling paper can be used.

About 25 sq. feet of *Masonite* or similar board are required for the house. General standard sizes of panels are 6 ft., 8 ft., 10 ft. and 12 ft. by 4 ft. With careful planning it should be possible to get the whole thing out of an 8 ft. by 4 ft. panel.

TOY PAINTING

TOYS SHOULD BE well finished, brilliantly coloured, with strong contrasts. There should be the fewest possible sharp corners, and the paint should dry perfectly hard so that it will not only tend to keep clean, but will admit of easy cleaning if it becomes necessary. With regard to the paint, so far as it is possible to arrange, it should be non-poisonous. About the only stipulation one could make in this respect is that it should be leadless. If we are not mistaken, the law enacts that all paints containing lead shall be so labelled. Ordinary house paints do not dry quickly enough or hard enough for the present purpose. Suitable paints in conveniently small quantities and a good range of colours are available in most general stores. Some are known as Chinese lacquers, others as synthetic enamels; there are many kinds, generally including the word "lac" in their name. *Valspar*, *Joy*, and *Japlac* give good results. Cellulose enamels are satisfactory, but not quite so easy to apply. The chief advantage with cellulose is that it dries in a few minutes.

Ready-mixed paints seldom need thinning, but a little white spirit (commonly called turpentine substitute) may be added if necessary. Cellulose paints need special thinners.

While on the subject of paints and thinners a word of warning would not be out of place. BEWARE OF FIRE. All paints are inflammable and cellulose particularly so. The kitchen table will generally be the work bench, in close proximity probably to the gas stove and boiler. An accident may happen; a pot of paint or thinners may be overturned and would catch fire immediately if it reached a flame. If cellulose materials are being used there should be no naked flame in the room—and this includes in a lesser degree the boiler.

A variety of materials may be used in the making of toys; wood, cardboard, tin, hardboard, and perhaps plaster. Those made of wood should be well glasspapered to remove sharp corners and make

FIG. 1. SCREW USED TO HOLD WORK WHILST BEING PAINTED

them generally smooth to the touch. All irregularities such as nail holes, splits, bad joints, rough wood, etc., are best filled with *Alabastine* and rubbed down perfectly smooth when dry. It would be wise to touch all nail heads with shellac before filling.

So far as toys are concerned, we can disregard the traditional methods of painting, i.e. priming, under-coating, and finishing. All that one needs to do is to apply a sealer to stop suction before using the finishing enamel. Size is satisfactory, but knotting or French polish is better. In many cases one coat of paint will be sufficient, but the lighter colours may need a second coat.

The difficulties when painting a small article are how to hold it while it is being painted, how to arrange to paint the whole at one sitting, and finally how to park it for drying without damage. It is often a good plan to paint part of the article and allow it to dry before painting the remainder. Another plan is to rest the partially painted toy on some upturned drawing pins and to complete the painting in that position. Sometimes a nail can be tapped in—in an out-of-the-way spot—which can be used for holding the toy while it is being painted and for suspension for drying. It might help if a number of panel pins were driven through a piece of plywood so that the painted articles could be rested gently on the points.

Sometimes there is a hole into which a large screw can be driven a few turns to provide a temporary handle (Fig. 1). In other cases it is necessary to drive in three or four nails, not only to enable the article to be handled, but also to keep it up from the table whilst drying. It is usually possible to insert these in an unnoticeable position. This is shown in Fig. 2.

PIN

FIG. 2. HOW PINS OR NAILS CAN
BE USED TO SUPPORT WORK
WHILST DRYING

As to suitable markings and colourings, the embryo toy painter would be well advised to take a walk through the toy department of one of the big stores and note schemes adopted by the professionals. Remember children are not interested in finicky detail; they like striking effects.

When several colours are being used in close proximity, it is wise to use the lighter tone first to avoid any difficulty in covering. For example, when painting a "Donald Duck" it would be better to paint the white eyes and the yellow parts first and allow them to dry before putting on the surrounding colours and the black segment in the eyes.

There is no particular need to adhere to natural colours where the very young children are concerned, but with the more outstanding common objects, such as railway engines, horses, dogs, cats, birds, etc., it is best to paint them so that the object in miniature may be associated with memories of the real thing.

Brushes for toy painting should be of good quality and not too large. Ordinary paint brushes will do for some work, but for the smaller toys it would be best to use those known as "camel hair". Despite the name they will probably be made of ox or squirrel hair. Artists' hog-hair fitches would be useful as they are of a better quality than ordinary paint brushes. For defining clear-cut edges and for small work it would be best to obtain one or two sable pencils. Always clean brushes immediately on completion of a painting session; wash them first in paraffin or turpentine, dry them well on paper, and then wash them well in soap and water.

Fine lines such as one sees on motor-cars, are often an improvement. Normally this work is done with special lining brushes or sword stripers, but a reasonably good substitute is a feather from a pigeon's wing. The tip of the feather should be used, held between the thumb and finger. The two middle fingers will serve as a guide against the edge of the article.

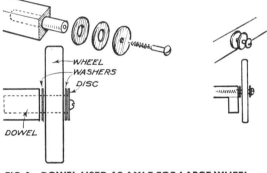

FIG. 3. DOWEL USED AS AXLE FOR LARGE WHEEL
FIG. 4. SMALL WHEEL PIVOTED ON SCREW

Old toys, tricycles, pedal-cars, etc., can be brought to new condition by repainting. The most important part of this work is the preparation. Every part must be thoroughly washed to remove all dirt, grease, and oil. After washing, the old paint should be well rubbed down with fine glasspaper to provide a grip for the new paint. New paint might flake off if applied to the hard, shiny surface of old enamel; and this would not do for toys which younger children are likely to put into their mouths. Before second coating rub down lightly with fine glasspaper.

One may be called upon to repaint a rocking horse. The traditional colour is known as dapple-grey. Contrary to a fairly common belief, it consists of light patches on a darker ground, and not vice versa. The general tone is a light dove grey, occasioned by a grey background being spotted with a much lighter grey, almost white. Here and there the white spots are more pronounced, being laid over a somewhat darker patch of grey. To paint a rocking horse then, one would need three tones of grey, made from white, black, and perhaps a touch of blue, and yellow; the lightest tone not much removed from white, the middle tone a dove colour, and the darkest one a slate colour. Paint a convenient section with the middle tone and blend in a large patch here and there with the darker grey. While the colour is still wet take a sponge and mottle with the light tone. Blend well with a dry brush to avoid any harshness. Over the darker patches the light spots can be somewhat larger. The mouth and nostrils are usually painted red, the eyes white with a black segment, and the hooves black.

One point to remember is that, although paint covers up the wood beneath, it cannot change its surface. That is to say that, if you leave the surface rough or uneven, the paint is going to be rough or uneven too. Always then finish off the wood well before beginning to paint. A cabinet finish may be unnecessary, but it should be reasonably good.

Any nail holes or other blemishes should be filled in with plastic wood or putty. The latter is cheaper, but plastic wood is very convenient. Allow plenty of time for it to dry off before cleaning up. If the hole is large, put in one layer and allow to set before finishing off. Otherwise the outside is liable to dry leaving the inside soft. Pile the filling above the hole because it is liable to shrink as it dries out.

Quite small toys can be painted with poster colours which are obtainable in a wide range of bright colours and have the advantage of drying quickly and of covering well. To fix them a coat of clear oil varnish should be given, or clear cellulose. The former takes longer to dry but is more durable, not being so brittle. Sometimes two coats are needed, especially over end grain.

GENERAL HINTS

Rounded corners. A most desirable feature in all toys is that all sharp edges and corners should be rounded over. The plane can be used for long edges and when a generous round is required. Otherwise the file or even glasspaper will take off the sharpness. Fittings with sharp corners, too, should be avoided. If necessary they can often be filed. Screws should be countersunk below the surface. Nails should always be punched in and care taken to see that there are no points projecting right through. When they are clenched see that the points are well in.

Incidentally, a nailed joint can be strengthened considerably by "dovetailing" the nails; that is, driving them in askew in alternate directions. Another useful tip is that nails always have a stronger grip when driven in across the grain rather than with it. This applies also to screws.

Wheels. These are always something of a problem. Various types can be obtained in both wood and metal, the latter being either of the pressed disc type or with spokes. The last named may be difficult to obtain, and for large toys, the only plan is to look round for some discarded pram wheels or make some in wood. Thick plywood is excellent for the purpose, but if this is not available solid wood can be used providing it is sound.

When the wheel is fairly large and has to withstand a fair amount of strain—when the child has to ride on the toy for instance—the best plan is to arrange an axle in the form of a fairly large dowel as shown in Fig. 3. A washer at each side reduces wear, and a disc at the outside held with a round-head screw prevents the whole thing from coming off. For smaller wheels the shank of the round-head screw can serve as the axle (Fig. 4). Note that washers are most desirable.